C000072259

BLUEBIRDS

VS.

JACKS

BLUEBIRDS START HERE

First published 2009
by Black & White Publishing Ltd
29 Ocean Drive, Edinburgh EH6 6JL

1 3 5 7 9 10 8 6 4 2   09 10 11 12 13

ISBN: 978 1 84502 281 5

Text © Ian Black 2009

The right of Ian Black to be identified as the author of this work has
been asserted by him in accordance with the Copyright, Designs and
Patents Act 1988.

All rights reserved. No part of this publication may be reproduced,
stored in a retrieval system, or transmitted in any form, or by any
means, electronic, mechanical, photocopying, recording or otherwise,
without permission in writing from the publisher.

A CIP catalogue record for this book is available from the British Library.

Typeset by RefineCatch Limited, Bungay, Suffolk
Printed and bound by CPI Cox & Wyman, Reading

INTRODUCTION

Every Bluebird worth his or her salt knows that talk is cheap in Swansea because supply exceeds demand and that the first question at a Swansea pub quiz is: "What are you looking at?" But not many know why the River Tawe runs through Swansea. The answer being of course that if it walked it would get mugged.

It has been asserted that Jacks are so dense that light bends around them and if you stand close enough to one, not that one would want to, but if you do, you can hear the sea.

You may learn within that parents from Blaenymaes in Swansea are incredibly hard, but they never smack their children. Well, maybe one or two grams to get them to sleep at night. CBS TV had planned to make a series of Crime Scene Investigation in Blaenymaes but plans were abandoned after realising that the entire population only has one tooth and that they all have the same DNA.

The song below is sung in Cardiff, and not just at football grounds. I've heard it sung in pubs late of an evening, when the beer is revealing the real feeling.

To the tune of "You Are My Sunshine":

You're just a Jack
A smelly Jack
You're only happy on Giro day
Your Ma's a stealer
Your Da's a dealer
Please don't take my hubcaps away.

Bluebirds know that in Jack families, father, mother and sister often don't add up to three, but that they do keep their knives sharp.

These are hard hits from the Bluebird side, digs, pokes in the eye, sharp jibes and bludgeoning diatribes, but it's just friendly rivalry really. Not.

Orraye? 'Ow's yer twll dyn for black'eads?

1

ATTITUDES AND INSULTS

A Bluebird, a former public schoolboy, says that though he could buy a mansion in Swansea and have a million or so left over by moving there, he wouldn't want to live in a city where, more often than not, the school uniform is wellies.

True tale from a Cardiff pavement cafe.

Bluebird: "It's a real shame that those ETA terrorists are bombing the Jacks in Benidorm."

Jack at next table: "But Bluebirds go to Benidorm as well."

Bluebird: "Not during the Swansea holidays we don't."

How do you know when you're staying in a hotel in Swansea?

When you call the receptionist and say "I've got a leak in my sink" and the response is "Fine, go ahead".

In Cardiff tables and chairs outside means a chance to have a seat and a chat over your coffee or beer. In Swansea, it's an eviction.

On the train from Swansea to Cardiff, a Jack was berating the Bluebird sitting across from him in the compartment. "You Bluebirds are too stuffy. You set yourselves apart too much. You think your stiff upper lips and your public schools make you above the rest of us. Takes you five generations to accept an immigrant. Look at me and my brothers and sisters. We have Italian blood, Russian blood, Jewish blood, Danish blood, and Swedish blood. What do you say to that?"

The Bluebird replied, "Your mother sounds like a very sporting lady."

Before the last World Cup, a primary school teacher in Cardiff asks her pupils if they want to see England win it. The full class put their hands up except for one girl who says she wants Sweden, or Trinidad and Tobago to win. Anyone, in fact, but England. Amazed, the teacher asks why.

"Well miss, my mum and dad are Scottish so I'm a Scottish fan too."

The teacher replies: "You don't have to be a Scotland fan because your parents are, if your mum was a prostitute and dad was a junkie that stole and beat up innocent people you wouldn't be like that."

"No miss," the girl says, "that would make me a Jack."

Two boys were playing football in the park when suddenly one of them is attacked by a Rottweiler.

Thinking quickly, his friend rips a plank of wood from a fence, forces it into the dog's collar and twists it, breaking the dog's neck.

All the while, a journalist from the South Wales Echo, who was taking a stroll through the park, is watching. He rushes over, introduces himself and takes out his pad and pencil to start his story for the next edition. He writes: "Brave Bluebird fan saves friend from vicious animal!"

The boy interrupts: "But I'm not a Scumdiff fan."

The reporter starts again: "Heroic rugby fan rescues friend from horrific attack!"

Again the boy interrupts: "But I'm not a rugby fan either."

"Who do you support then?" inquires the reporter.

"Swansea," comes the reply.

So the reporter starts again: "Jack bastard murders family pet."

Your average Jack is a sort of one-man or one-woman slum. Inside and out.

2

DREAMING OF A JACK CHRISTMAS

To the tune of "Mistletoe and Wine"

Christmas time, drunkenness and crime,
Children playing – in filth and grime,
With cars on fire – and radios from them
Time to rejoice – in be-ing Jack,
It's a time for stealing, a time for receiving,
Knock-off stuff – what a great feelin'
Why pay top dollar – you can nick it for free,
Just like our electricity, gas and TV

Christmas time, pissups all the time
Nicking fags – spirits and wine
Wearing shell-suits and Nikes – all knocked off gear
It's great getting pissed – on someone else's beer
Its a time for drinkin' – six packs of Stella
That you got – from some dodgy fella
Christmas is sound – Christmas is best
God bless our dealer – and the DHSS
Christmas time – time to joy-ride
Then go and visit – family inside

With Dad on a six stretch – and Sis up the duff
This City of Swansea can get pretty rough

So next time your driving – through Jack-city
You may just know why – the streets look so shitty
So keep a sharp eye out – for those dodgy deals
If you park for two minutes, they're off with your
    wheels

3

YOU CAN STICK SEBASTIAN COE UP YOUR TWLL DYN

Swansea are to bid to host 2012 Olympics, removing it from London, as it is costing us a fortune and we are getting sod all from it, bit like the government, really.

In an attempt to influence the members of the International Olympic Committee on their choice of venue for the games the organisers of Swansea's bid have drawn up an itinerary and schedule of events. A copy has been leaked and is reproduced below.

Opening Ceremony – The Olympic flame will be ignited by a petrol bomb thrown by a native of the city (probably from the Townhill area), wearing the traditional costume of shell suit, baseball cap and balaclava mask. It will burn for the duration of the games in a large chip van situated on the roof of the stadium.

The Events – In previous Olympic games, Britain's competitors have not been particularly successful. In order to redress the balance, some of the events have been altered slightly to the advantage of local athletes:

100 Metres Sprint – Competitors will have to hold a video recorder and microwave oven (one under each arm) and on the sound of the starting pistol, a police dog will be released from a cage 10 yards behind the athletes.

100 Metres Hurdle – As above but with added obstacles (i.e. car bonnets, hedges, garden fences, walls, etc.)

Hammer – Competitors may choose the type of hammer they wish to use (claw, sledge, etc) the winner will be the one who can cause the most grievous bodily harm to members of the public within the time allowed.

Fencing – Entrants will be asked to dispose of as much stolen silver and jewellery as possible in five minutes.

Shooting – A strong challenge is expected from the local men in this event. The first target will be a moving police car, the next a post office van and then a Securicor wages vehicle.

Boxing – Entry to the boxing will be restricted to husband and wife teams, and will take place on a Friday night. The husband will be given 15 pints of Brains, while the wife will be told not to make him any tea when he gets home. The bout will then commence.

Cycling Time Trials – Competitors will break into the University bike sheds and take an expensive mountain bike owned by some mummy's boy from the country on his first trip away from home. All against the clock.

Cycling Pursuit – As above but the bike will belong to a visiting member of the Australian rugby team who will witness the theft.

Modern Pentathlon – Amended to include mugging, breaking and entering, flashing, joy-riding and arson.

The Marathon – A safe route has yet to be decided, but competitors will be issued with bags full of litter which they will distribute on their way round the course.

Swimming – Competitors will be thrown into the Tawe. The first three survivors back will decide the medals.

Men's 50km Walk – Unfortunately this event will have to be cancelled as police cannot guarantee the safety of anyone walking the streets of Swansea.

Closing Ceremony – Entertainment will include formation rave dancing by members of Swansea Health in the Community anti-drug campaigners, synchronised rock throwing, and music by Goldie Lookin Chain. The Olympic flame will be extinguished by someone dropping an old washing machine onto it from the top floor of the block of flats next to the stadium. The stadium will then be boarded up before the local athletes break into it and remove all the copper piping and the central heating boiler.

4

JACK OFFS

Jimmy the Jack was awarded £10,000 for injuries received after a traffic accident and his wife got £2,000. A friend asked how badly injured his wife had been in the accident.

He replied, "She wasn't hurt at all but I had the presence of mind to break her leg before the police arrived."

Jacks love animals. They taste great.

The Jack got lost in thought. It was unfamiliar territory.

Some people have a photographic memory. Some Jacks just don't have film.

There's many a Swansea man with the heart of a little child. They usually keep them in jars.

There are two theories about arguing with Jacks. Neither of them works.

Cardiff omelette: First, borrow four eggs.
Swansea omelette: First, steal four eggs.

5

ARE YOU LIVING TOO CLOSE TO SWANSEA?

Below are some tell-tale signs:

1. Your spouse has a poster of Alan Tate smiling as a role model.

2. You let your 12-year-old daughter smoke at the dinner table in front of her kids.

3. You've been married three times and still have the same in-laws.

4. You think that a woman is "out of your league" because she asks for a glass with her Buckfast.

5. The phrase "Thunderbirds are go!" reminds you the off licence has just opened.

6. You wish your toilet at home could be as "clean" as the one in the bus station.

7. Anyone in your family ever died right after saying, "Hey! Watch this."

8. You think Dom Perignon is a Mafia leader.

9. Your wife's hairdo was once ruined by a ceiling fan.

10. Your school had a students' creche.

11. One, or more, of your kids was born on a pub pool table.

12. One, or more, of your kids was conceived on a pub pool table.

13. Your back door coal bunker is ideal for the Rottweiler to raise its pups.

14. The trade-in value of your transit goes up and down, depending on how full the tank is.

15. You don't have to leave the house to put rubbish in the wheelie bin.

16. You once lit a match in the bathroom and the windows blew out.

17. You only need one more stamp on your card to get a freebie at "Tom's Tattoos".

18. You can't get married to your childhood sweet-heart because of the current bestiality laws.

19. You think "loading a dishwasher", means getting your wife drunk.

20. Your toilet paper has page numbers on it.

and finally . . .

21. The soundtrack on your wedding video ends with the loudhailer message:
"THIS IS THE POLICE."

6

SWANSEA FOLK: CAN'T LIVE WITH THEM AND IT IS NOW ILLEGAL TO KILL THEM.

Santa Claus, the tooth fairy, an intelligent Jack and an old drunk are walking down the street together when simultaneously they each spot a 50 pound note.

Who gets it?

The old drunk, of course. The other three are mythological.

A father takes his young son to the zoo where they are fascinated by the lions.

"Daddy, Daddy, why is that lion licking his bum?" asks the boy.

"Son, that's because he has just eaten a Jack and is trying to get rid of the taste."

Q: How do you get four old ladies in Swansea to swear?

A: Get the fifth old woman to shout: "Bingo!"

Bluebird to Jack: "You are depriving some poor village of its idiot."

The purchasing agent of a big company was a stuffy old Bluebird, but he gave an extensive order to a Jack salesman. Although he had won the business in open competition, the salesman was grateful at being chosen and sought a way to show it. He knew he daren't offer the buyer a commission, and a gift of money, he thought, would be regarded by him as an insult. The man, he noticed, constantly smoked cigars.

So the salesman slipped out to a cigar shop and bought a box of 50 of the finest Havanas the tobacconist had. The price for the 50 was £500, but it had been a really big order that he had won. He brought the box back and asked the buyer to accept it with his compliments.

The latter explained that it was against company policy for its buyers to accept presents of any sort from those with whom the firm did business. He was sorry, he said, but he could not take the cigars as a present, even though he felt sure his young friend had given them with the best of intentions and in absolute good faith.

The young Jack had another idea:

"Well," he said, "I hate to throw these cigars away. They are of no use to me – I don't even smoke cigarettes. I wonder if you would buy them from me? There's no harm in that, surely."

"What would you be asking for them?" inquired the Bluebird.

"I'll sell the whole 50 to you for a fiver," stated the salesman.

The buyer lifted one of the cigars from the top row, smelled it, rolled it in his fingers an eyed it closely.

"Okay," he said, "at that price I'll take four boxes."

Cardiff threat: I'll wring your neck, you little Jack bastard, but only if you wash it.

Badge spotted in one of Swansea's fine call centres: "I'm just working here until a good fast food job opens up."

How many Jack flies does it take to screw in a light bulb?
Only two, but you have to wonder how the sneaky little bastards got in there.

Jack Compliments:
'Er, she could shoplift in a kebab shop.

At the conclusion of a more than satisfactory repast: "I've eaten worse."

You want to feel really handsome, svelte and successful? Go shopping at Tesco in Swansea.

What's the difference between a Jack and a sperm?
A sperm has one chance in ten million of becoming a human being.

How many Jacks does it take to change a light bulb?
It doesn't matter, they're all condemned to eternal darkness anyway.

What do you get when you cross a Jack with a pig?
I don't know. There are some things a pig just won't do.

What's the difference between a wedding and a wake in Swansea?
There's one less drunk at a wake.

Q. Why wasn't Jesus born in Swansea?
A. Because God couldn't find three wise men and a virgin.

Why are they putting Jacks at the bottom of the sea?
    They found out that deep down, they're really not so bad.

Two Jacks jump off a cliff, which one hits the ground first?
Who gives a fuck?

Jacks:
    Got into the gene pool when the lifeguard wasn't looking.
    One-celled organisms out-score them in IQ tests.
    Prime candidates for natural deselection.

Dead Jacks: why aren't there more?

7

SCHOOL DAZE

Jack teachers are known to use the following translations for the remarks they make on pupils' report cards:

"A born leader" – Runs a protection racket

"Easy-going" – Bone idle

"Good progress" – You should have seen him a year ago

"Friendly" – Never shuts up

"Helpful" – A creep

"Reliable" – Informs on his friends

"Expresses himself confidently" – Impertinent

"Enjoys physical education" – A bully

"Does not accept authority easily" – Dad is in prison

"Often appears tired" – Stays up all night watching television

"A rather solitary child" – He smells

"Popular in the playground" – Sells pornography

The young Jack's report card said: "At last some good news. We thought Wayne had reached rock bottom.

But now he has developed a hitherto unsuspected talent for digging."

The same teacher a year later said: "The dawn of legibility in Wayne's handwriting has revealed his utter inability to spell."

8

LAZY, UGLY AND STUPID. WITH SHEEPSHAGGING

Jacks are so lazy that they won't marry a woman till she's pregnant.

A Swansea wife gets on to the bus holding her three-week-old baby.

The bus driver says: "Hey, your baby is the ugliest baby I've ever seen!"

The woman pays her fare and goes off and sits up the back of the bus almost in tears.

A man says to her: "What's up, bach?"

She says: "The bus driver has just been very rude to me."

The man replies: "Although you are a filthy Jack, you shouldn't let him get away with that, I reckon you should go and say something. He is a public servant and he can't do that to you."

She says: "I will then, I'm off."

The Cardiff man then says: "Do you want me to hold your monkey?"

Two Jacks are standing on a cliff. One has two budgies on his shoulder, the other has a parrot on his. The first Jack jumps and goes screaming through the air to land in a crumpled heap on the ground below.

Seconds later, his mate jumps. Halfway down, he pulls out a pistol and blows the parrot's head off, but to no avail, as he crashes in a heap next to his mate.

First Jack moans, then says to his mate: "This budgie-jumping is overrated."

His mate half-turns his broken neck and replies: "Yes, and the parrot-shooting isn't much better."

What do you call a sheep tied to a lamp-post in Swansea?

A leisure centre.

A Jack was out for a walk and came to a river and saw a Bluebird on the opposite bank.

"Hello there," she shouts, "how can I get to the other side?"

The Jack looked up the river, then down the river, then shouted back, "You ARE on the other side."

9

BLUEBIRDS AND DRINK

John the Bluebird reckoned he was a great judge of a glass of whisky – and a merciless executioner.

Gavin the Bluebird was sitting at the bar drinking double whiskies in one gulp as fast as the barman could put them in front of him. He eventually explained that it was the only way he could drink them after a terrible accident.

"What sort of accident?" asked the barman.

"Terrible," said Gavin. "I knocked one over with my elbow."

The minister of a church in one of the more salubrious districts of Cardiff was preaching a strong sermon about the evils of drink, and kept telling the congregation not to imbibe too frequently.

He concluded: "We'll not make this sermon too personal, but if a short, bald-headed chap who owns a chain of video shops, two restaurants and a pub, and is sitting in the corner of the east gallery pew, takes it to heart, then the Lord surely does work in mysterious ways."

10

JUST DESSERTS

A Bluebird and a Jack are walking along a beach when they see an old bottle.

The Jack picks it up and takes out the cork.

Out pops a genie who says, "I am the genie with the light brown hair. I will grant you three wishes each."

"OK then," the Jack says, "I wish every person in Swansea was female apart from me."

"I'd like a Ferrari," says the Bluebird.

The Jack, wanting better than the Bluebird says, "I wish everyone in Europe was female apart from me."

"I'd like a garage for my Ferrari," says the Bluebird.

"I wish everyone in the world was female apart from me," says the Jack.

"I wish the Jack to be gay!" says the Bluebird.

11

THIEVING JACKS

If you see a Jack on a bicycle, why should you never swerve to hit him?
  It could be your bike.

A Bluebird woman said that whenever someone from Cardiff wears something expensive, it looks old, and when a Jack does so, it looks stolen.

What is the difference between Batman and a Jack?
  Batman can go out without robbin'.

What did the little Jack boy get for Christmas?
  Your bike.

12

TERRACING TALK

We're Bluebirds, we're insane,
We drink Brains and sniff cocaine,
With a nick knack paddy wack give the dog
a bone,
Why don't Swansea fuck off home?

To the tune of "Hey Baby"

Heeeey Jacks! Ooh ah,
I wanna kno-oo-oo-ow where's my video . . .
and my stereo and my dvd . . .
and my granny's purse.

13

BLUEBIRD PHILOSOPHY

Cardiff question: If you try to fail, and succeed, which have you done?

Cardiff saying: Laugh alone and the world thinks you're an idiot.

Cardiff prayer: "God bless Cardiff. And God, we've got to flit to Swansea tomorrow. So, goodbye, God."

In Cardiff they say: "Opportunities are never lost; someone will always take the one you missed."

In Swansea they say: "Do you mean oppurchancities?"

A closed mouth gathers no feet, as they say in Cardiff.

Cardiff saying: Give me ambiguity or give me something else.

The Bluebirds way of saying "No" is to start a conservation group.

14

HEAVEN

"Heaven seems not all that much better than Swansea," a Jack is said to have confided, after death, to a friend who had died before him.

"Dai buttie, this isn't Heaven," replied his pal.

A man from Cardiff, a Scouser and a Jack wound up together at the Pearly Gates. St Peter informed them that in order to get into Heaven, they would each have to answer one question.

St Peter addressed the Bluebird and asked, "What was the name of the ship that crashed into the iceberg?"

He answered quickly, "That would be the Titanic." St Peter let him through the gate.

St Peter turned to the Scouser and, thinking that Heaven didn't need all the attitudes that this guy would bring with him, decided to make the question a little harder: "How many people died on the ship?"

Fortunately for him, he had seen the movie and answered, "About 1,500."

"That's right! You may enter."

St Peter then turned to the Jack: "Name them."

15

HELL

A Bluebird, a Jack and a Scouser found themselves in hell. They were a little confused at their situation, and they were startled to see a door in the wall open. Behind the door was perhaps the ugliest woman they had ever seen.

She was 3 ft 4 in, dirty, and you could smell her even over the brimstone.

The voice of the Devil was heard: "Scouser, you have sinned! You are condemned to spend the rest of eternity in bed with this woman!"

He was then whisked through the door by a group of lesser demons to his torment.

This understandably shook up the other two, and so they both jumped when a second door opened, and they saw an even more disgusting example of womanhood gone wrong. She was over 7 ft tall, monstrous, covered in thick black hair, and flies circled her.

The voice of the Devil was heard: "Bluebird, you have sinned! You are condemned to spend the rest of eternity in bed with this woman!" And he too was whisked off.

The Jack, now alone, felt understandably anxious and feared the worst when the third door opened. As it inched open, he strained to see the figure of . . . Paris Hilton.

Delighted, the Jack jumped up, taking in the sight of this beautiful woman, barely dressed in a skimpy bikini. Then he heard the voice of the Devil saying: "PARIS, YOU HAVE SINNED . . ."

16

SWANSEA FANS

Swansea's kit for next season has just been unveiled. It's all-white with a pointed white hood and a flaming cross on the front.

Swansea's manager was looking to sign some new players to help Swansea's title push, so he sent his chief scout to Iraq to search for some new talent. Sure enough, the scout finds an outstanding 18-year-old striker and immediately signs him on a three-year deal.

On getting back to Wales the manager takes one look at him in training and immediately puts him in the starting line up for the big away game against Cardiff.

The new lad is fantastic, he scores a hat trick and creates four more as Swansea romp it 7–0. Ecstatic after the game, the young lad phones his mum to tell her the good news.

"Mum" he says, "I've just made my debut and had a great game. The team loves me, the fans love me and the press loves me, even them twats on the radio phone-in love me. Life is great!"

"Well," says his mum, "I'm glad life is great for you. Shall I tell you what happened to us today? Your Dad's been murdered in the street, your sister and I were raped and beaten in broad daylight, and your brother's joined a vicious gang of killers."

"Mum, I don't know what to say. I'm so sorry."

"Sorry?" She yells down the phone. "You're fucking sorry? It's your fucking fault we moved to Swansea in the first place!"

How many Swansea fans does it take to change a light bulb?

Seven – one to change it, five to moan about it and the coach to say that if the ref had done his job in the first place the light bulb would never have gone out.

An anxious woman goes to her doctor.

"Doctor," she asks nervously, "I'm a bit worried – can you get pregnant from anal intercourse?"

"Of course," replies the doctor, "Where do you think Swansea fans come from?"

A scientist is researching the effects of the loss of brain power on people's speech. So he brings in a guy off the street to participate in the experiments.

As they attach the electrodes to his head, the guy says, "May I please have a drink of water?"

But the scientist ignores him and says to his assistant, "Remove 25 percent of his brain power now."

The assistant does this and the guy then says, "Give me water."

Again the scientist ignores him and says, "Remove another 25 percent."

Guy: "Give drink water."

Scientist: "Now another 25 percent."

Guy: "Wawa, wawa."

Scientist: "And now, the final 25 percent."

Guy (singing): "Come on Swansea . . ."

A Swansea fan is trapped on a remote desert island with a sheep and a dog. Soon, the sheep starts looking really attractive to the Swansea fan. However, whenever he approaches the sheep the dog growls in a threatening manner.

The Swansea fan takes the dog to the opposite side of the island giving it some food as a distraction. He runs back to the sheep only to find the dog growling at him. The Swansea fan ties the dog to a tree with a large leash. He goes back to the sheep only to find the dog growling with a gnawed off leash around its neck.

By now, the Swansea fan is getting depressed and frustrated. As he sits under a palm tree staring out to sea, a beautiful woman in a tight-fitting wet suit emerges from the surf.

She asks him who he is and, taking pity upon his lonely state, asks if there's anything at all she could do for him.

The Swansea fan thinks for a moment and then responds, "Could you take the dog for a walk?"

Two Swansea-supporting farmers are flying with their herd of sheep to a new farm.

Suddenly, the plane engine fails and it rapidly descends towards the ground.

First fan: "Quick! Grab a parachute and jump."

Second fan: "What about the sheep?"

First fan: "Fuck the sheep!"

Second fan, after a pause: "Do you think we have time?"

Q: What do you call a Swansea fan with five sheep?

A: A pimp.

17

RECOGNISE ANY JACKS YOU KNOW?

All booster, no payload.

All crown, no filling.

All foam, no beer.

All hammer, no nail.

All he remembers about his middle name is the first letter.

All his eggs in the same basket.

All his learning curves look like Mount Everest.

All icing, no cake.

All the lights don't shine in her marquee.

Always in the right place, but at the wrong time.

Always loses battles of wits because he's unarmed.

Always sharpening his sleeping skills.

An experiment in Artificial Stupidity.

An expert on the historical significance of cottage cheese.

An inch short and a stroke early.

18

MENTAL WELLNESS

NHS cutbacks are going a bit far. This is, allegedly, the message you receive when you phone Cefn Coed Hospital:

"Hello, you have reached the Psychiatric Clinic.

If you are obsessive-compulsive, press 1 repeatedly.

If you are co-dependent, have someone press 2 for you.

If you are paranoid, we know who you are. Stay on the line so we can trace this call.

If you suffer from multiple personality disorder, press 3, 4 and 5.

If you are suffering from a schizophrenic personality disorder, wait for a little voice to tell you which number to press.

If you are paranoid-delusional, we know who you are and what you want. Just stay on the line so we can trace the call.

If you are depressed, it doesn't matter which number you press. No one will answer. Ever.

If you are delusional and occasionally hallucinate, please be aware that the thing you are holding to the side of your head is alive and about to bite your ear off."

The psychology instructor at Singleton had just finished a lecture on mental health and was giving an oral test.

Speaking specifically about manic depression, she asked: "How would you diagnose a patient who walks back and forth screaming at the top of his lungs one minute, then sits in a chair weeping uncontrollably the next?"

A Jack at the back raised his hand and asked: "Cardiff's Manager?"

19

ANOTHER WORD TO THE WISE

This is a real sign in a Swansea shop:

"Warning to shoplifters: Anyone caught shoplifting will be gagged, beaten, whipped and tortured. Any survivors will be prosecuted to the full extent of the law."

20

JACK LORD'S PRAYER

Our Lager,
Which art in barrels,
Hallowed be thy drink.
Thy will be drunk (I will be drunk),
At home, as it is in the pub.
Give us this day our foamy head,
And forgive us our spillages,
As we forgive those who spill against us.
And lead us not to incarceration,
But deliver us from hangovers.
For thine is the beer, the ale and the lager,
For ever and ever,
Barmen.

21

PLAIN SAILING

A keen Jack lad applied for a salesman's job. The supervisor asked him, "Have you ever been a salesman before?"

He replied confidently that he had. The guy liked the cut of his jib and said, "You can start tomorrow and I'll come and see you when we close up."

The day was long and arduous for the young man, but finally five o'clock came around. The supervisor duly turned up and asked: "How many sales did you make today?"

"One," said the Jack.

"Only one?" he said. "Most of the staff make 20 or 30 sales a day. How much was the sale worth?"

"Three hundred thousand pounds," said the young man with a cheeky Jack grin.

"How did you manage that?" asked the flabbergasted boss.

"Well," said the salesman, "this guy came in and I sold him a little fish hook, then a medium hook and finally a really big hook. Then I sold him a small fishing line, a medium one and a huge big one.

I asked him where he was going fishing and he said down the coast. I said he would probably need a boat, so I took him down to the boat department and sold him that 20-footer with the twin engines. Then he said his Volkswagen probably wouldn't be able to pull it, so I took him to the car department and sold him a great big four-wheeler."

The supervisor took two steps back and asked in astonishment: "You sold all that to a guy who came in for a fish hook?"

"No," answered the Jack: "He came in to buy a box of Tampax for his wife and I said to him, 'Your weekend's knackered. You might as well go fishing.' "

22

TRUE STORY

A Jack school teacher injured his back over the summer holidays and had to wear a plaster cast around the upper part of his body. It fitted neatly under his shirt and was not noticeable at all.

On the first day of his new school, still with the cast under his shirt, he found himself assigned to the worst behaved class in the school in one of Cardiff's worst estates.

He walked into the rowdy classroom, opened the window as wide as possible and then busied himself with desk work. When a strong breeze made his tie flap, he took the stapler from his desk and stapled the tie to his chest. Oddly, he had no trouble with discipline that year, and for the next few years he was known as The Iron Jack.

23

ARSEHOLE, LOOPHOLE

What's the definition of a good Cardiff accountant?
Someone who has a loophole named after him.

Collective noun: A Wunch of Bankers

A torn-arsed Jack in trackies walks into a Cardiff bank and says to the female teller: "I want to open a fuckin' account."

To which the woman replied: "I beg your pardon, what did you say?"

"Listen, I said I want to open a fuckin' account right now."

"I'm sorry sir, but we do not tolerate that kind of language in this bank," she replied.

Then the woman left her desk and went through to the bank manager and told him about her situation. They both returned and the manager asked: "What seems to be the problem here?"

"There's no bastard problem," the man said, "I just won 16 million quid in the lottery and I want to open a fuckin' account at this fuckin' bank!"

"I see, sir," the manager said, "and this fucking bitch is giving you grief?"

24

PLUS ÇA CHANGE

A returned Swan exile gets in a taxi at the airport and asks to be taken into town. He falls into conversation, as you do, with the taxi driver, and winds up claiming that even after 20 years away he can still recognise Swansea districts by their smell and by how the air feels.

The driver takes up the challenge and produces a blindfold. (As they do, if asked.) They reach the first district and the guy opens the window, sticks his hand out, finger and thumb rubbing the air, takes a deep breath and says: "Gowerton."

He is of course right and the taxi driver asks: "How do you do that?"

The guy says: "Oh, I can feel that edge of capitalist competition, that 'I must keep up with the Joneses', bigger car, better house. Not too pleasant. Bit like Cardiff."

The driver then takes him to another district and the guy goes through the same procedure, sticking his arm out etc and says: "Townhill," then explains: "I can feel all of the nationalities that came here seeking refuge from torture, imprisonment and death in their former countries, their aspirations for their children, the hope that they will be accepted as new Jacks. I wish them well."

The driver is impressed and decides on one final test for the passenger. They get there and one second after he has stuck his hand out and before he has even taken a breath, he says: "Blaenymaes."

The driver says: "Jees, that was quick. How can you possibly know?"

The guy says: "My watch is gone."

Bluebirds who wish to convert this story to their native city have a wide choice of final district. You know where they are.

25

JACKS DO GRASS

One afternoon a wealthy Bluebird lawyer was driving home from a hard day robbing Jacks when he saw two men along the roadside eating grass. Curious, he stopped and got out to investigate.

"Why are you eating grass?" he asked one man.

"We don't have any money for food," said the guy, "so we have to eat grass."

"Well then, you can come with me to my house and I'll feed you," the Bluebird said.

"But I have a wife and two children. They're over there underneath that tree," said the guy pathetically.

"That's fine," replies the lawyer. "Bring them along too."

Turning to the other poor soul he stated: "You can come with us too."

The second man, in a pitiful voice, said, "But I have a wife and SIX children with me, some of them mine."

"Don't worry about it," the lawyer replies casually. "You can bring them along as well."

They all entered the car, which was no easy task, as even the vast 4¥4 nearly wasn't quite big enough. Once underway, one of the poor guys turned to the lawyer and said, "You are very kind, new friend. Thank you for taking all of us with you."

The Bluebird replied, "Glad to do it. You'll love my place. The grass is nearly a foot high!"

26

ANOTHER COUPLE FROM THE TERRACES

Build a bonfire,
Build a bonfire,
Put the Jacks on the top,
Put the city in the middle,
And then burn the fucking lot.

Feed the Jacks,
Let them know it's Christmas time,
Feed the Jacks,
Let them know it's Christmas time, etc.

Tune: "In Me Liverpool Home"

In your Swansea slums,
You look in the dustbin for something to eat,
You find a dead rat and you think it's a treat,
In your Swansea slums.

In your Swansea slums,
You shit on the carpet, you piss in the bath,
You finger your grandma, and think it's a laugh,
In your Swansea slums.

In your Swansea slums,
You speak in an accent that's thankfully rare,
You wear a pink tracksuit and have curly hair,
In your Swansea slums.

In your Swansea slums,
Your mum's on the game and your dad's in the nick,
You can't get a job 'cos you're too fucking thick,
In your Swansea slums.

27

LITTLE DARLINGS

The Jack teacher gave her class an exercise: Get their parents to tell them a story with a moral.

The next day the kids came back and one by one began to tell their stories.

"Johnny, do you have a story to share?"

"Yes, miss, my daddy told me a story about my Auntie Mel.

Auntie Mel was a pilot in Iraq and her plane was hit. She had to bail out over enemy territory and all she had were two bottles of Buckfast, a gun and a survival knife.

She drank the Buckfast on the way down so it would not break and then her parachute landed her right in the middle of 20 enemy troops.

She shot 15 of them with the gun until she ran out of bullets and killed four more with the knife till the blade broke and then she killed the last Iraqi with her bare hands and her teeth, biting his throat out."

"Jesus!" said the horrified teacher. "What kind of moral did your daddy tell you from that horrible story?"

Johnny replied: "Stay well away from Auntie Mel when she's been drinking."

Little Jack Billy walked into the house shortly before noon.

"Billy!" his mother cried. "What are you doing home from school so early?"

"I got the right answer to the question."

Beaming, his mother asked: "Which question was that?"

"Who put the dog shit on the teacher's chair? It was me."

28

THE LORD GOD AND JACKS

Standing on the shore, a Jack lady watches her grandson playing with the rubbish in the water. She is thunderstruck when she sees a huge wave crash over him. When it recedes, the boy is no longer there. He has vanished.

Screaming, the woman holds her hands to the sky and cries, "Lord, how could you? Have I not been a wonderful mother and grandmother? Have I not scrimped and saved so I could give to the church? Have I not always put others before myself? Have I not always turned my other cheek and loved my neighbours? Have I not –"

A deep, loud Bluebird voice from the sky interrupts. "Moan, moan, moan, moan. Give us a break, here!"

Immediately, another huge wave appears and crashes on the beach. And when it recedes, the boy is there, smiling and splashing around as if nothing ever happened.

The deep loud voice continues, "There's your lad back. Are you happy now?"

The Jack lady responded: "He had a hat."

29

ERUDITE INSULTS

If you live in Swansea, then being awake is not necessarily a desirable state.

In Swansea, you're considered posh if you have slates on your roof. Indeed, if you have a roof.

If you take a picture of a Jack, he runs about claiming you've stolen his soul.

30

DRY HUMOUR

Two Jacks are walking down the road in Cardiff when they see a sign in a shop window: Suits £15.00, Shirts £2.00, Trousers £2.50.

One said to the other one: "Look at that – we could buy a lot of that gear and, when we get back to Swansea, we could make a fortune. When we go into the shop don't say anything, let me do all the talking, cause if they hear our accent they might not serve us, so I'll speak in my best Cardiff voice."

They go in and he orders, in his best attempt at a Cardiff voice, 50 suits at £15.00, 100 shirts at £2.00 and 50 trousers at £2.50. The owner of the shop says: "You two are Jacks, aren't you?"

The Jack replies: "Yes, ok, how the hell did you know that?"

The owner says: "This is a dry cleaners."

31

SWANSEA WOMEN

Sean Connery was interviewed by Michael Parkinson, and bragged that despite his 78-years of-age, he could still have sex five times a night. Catherine Zeta Jones, who was also a guest, looked intrigued.

After the show, Catherine said: "Sean, if I'm not being too forward, I'd love to have sex with an even older man than my husband. Let's go back to my place."

So they go back to her place and have great sex. Afterwards, Sean says, "If you think that was good, let me shleep for half an hour, and we can have even better shex. But while I'm shleeping, hold my baws in your left hand and my wullie in your right hand."

Catherine looks a bit perplexed, but says, "Okay."

He sleeps for half an hour, awakens, and they have even better sex. Then Sean says, "Catherine, that was wonderful. But if you let me shleep for an hour, we can have the besht shex yet. But again, hold my baws in your left hand, and my wullie in your right hand."

Catherine is now used to the routine and complies. The results are mind blowing. It happens five times.

Once it's all over, and the cigarettes are lit, Catherine asks, "Sean, tell me, does me holding your balls in my left hand and your willie in my right stimulate you while you are sleeping?"

Sean replies, "No, it's just that the lasht time I shlept with a Swansea girl, she shtole my wallet."

What do you call a Jack woman with one leg?
Eileen.

32

MORE DUMB JACKS

The prosecution and defence had both presented their final arguments in a case involving a Jack accused of operating an illegal still.

The judge turned to the jury and asked: "Before giving you your instructions, do any of you have any questions?"

"Yes, M'lud," replied one of the jurors, a fellow estate dweller. "Did the defendant boil the malt one or two hours, how does he cool it quickly, and at what point does he add the yeast?"

Bluebird: "Did you ever hear that joke about the museum in Cardiff that had a skull of Queen Elizabeth the First when she was 12 in one room, and a skull when she was 30 in another?"

"No," said the Jack. "What was it?"

James and Jack the Jacks went into The Bank Statement in great good humour and ordered two large whiskies.

"Are you lads celebrating something?" asked the bartender.

"We are," said Jimmy. "We've just finished a jigsaw puzzle in record time. A hundred pieces it had, and it only took us six months."

"Six months? But that's quite a long time," said the bartender.

"I don't think so," said Jack. "It said on the box, three to five years."

33

GOLF

"Sandy, you promised to be home at two o'clock this afternoon and now it's after six."

"Bonny wife, please. That Jack I drew in the Medal is dead – dropped dead on the fourth green this morning."

"Oh, how terrible."

"It certainly was. The whole day, it's been: hit the ball . . . drag the Jack . . . hit the ball . . . drag the Jack."

34

CARDIFF'S FINEST

One of Cardiff's finest pulls over a Jack who's been weaving in and out of the lanes. He goes up to the man's window and says: "Sir, I need you to blow into this breathalyser tube."

The man says, "Sorry, orifice, I can't do that. I am an asthmatic. If I do that, I'll have a really bad asthma attack."

"Okay, fine. I need you to come down to the station to give a blood sample."

"I can't do that either. I am a haemophiliac. If I do that, I'll bleed to death."

"Well, then, we need a urine sample."

"I'm sorry, officer, I can't do that either. I am also a diabetic. If I do that, I'll get really low blood sugar."

"All right, then I need you to come out here and walk this white line."

"I can't do that either, orifice."

"Why not?"

"Because I'm absolutely fuckin' drunk."

A Jack lay sprawled across three entire stall seats in the New Theatre. When the usher came by and noticed this, he whispered to the man: "Sorry, sir, but you're only allowed one seat."

The man heard and looked up, but didn't budge.

The usher became impatient. "Sir, if you don't get up from there I'm going to have to call the manager."

This time the man made a gutteral sound, a very Jack noise, which infuriated the usher, who turned and marched briskly back up the aisle in search of his manager. In a few moments, both the usher and the manager returned and stood over the man. Together the two of them tried repeatedly to move him, but with no success.

Finally, they summoned the police.

The large sub-unit of Cardiff's Finest surveyed the situation briefly then asked: "All right, my friend, what's your name?"

"James," the man muttered.

"Oho," said the cop, having detected the Jack accent. "Where are you from, James?"

With pain in his voice James replied: "The balcony."

Late one Friday night the policeman spotted a Swansea man driving very erratically through the streets of Cardiff. They pulled the man over and asked him if he had been drinking that evening.

"Yes, I have. It's Friday, you know, and I'm in a foreign city, so I stopped by a pub where I had six or seven pints. And then there was something called 'Happy Hour' and they served these huge voddies for pennies. I had four or five of them. Then I stopped on the way home to get another bottle for later. I've drunk some already." And the man fumbled around in his jacket until he located his bottle of vodka, which he held up for inspection.

The officer sighed and said, "Sir, I'm afraid I'll need you to step out of the car and take a breathalyser test."

The Jack said indignantly: "Why? Don't you believe me?"

35

RANTS

Here's a young man who knows his own mind. He prefers to remain anonymous. There, there, let's go for a little lie down.

Swansea is a city that likes to boast about how culturally important it is, despite the fact that the only things to come out of Swansea are criminals and fucking Dylan Thomas. It seems to be a Jack law that whenever you go outside Swansea, you must always tell everyone who looks at you that it is the funniest place on earth, full of the nicest people. I suspect this is a ploy to get more unsuspecting visitors for mugging. In reality, Swansea is an absolute shithole, a city that seems to be held together using only graffiti, vomit and stacks of torn rubbish bags with the occasional used nappy that has been run over in the middle of the road. NOTHING funny EVER came out of Swansea.

And don't get me started on the accent. Jacks do not speak English. They actually speak some strange Klingon dialect from a place where everyone has chronic bronchitis. Swansea truly is the sphincter of this planet, and any colonic irrigation should be sent their way as soon as possible. I fucking hate Swansea and I hope that this little rant has somehow helped me to overcome the years of torture I had to go through constantly going there with my family. I hate it, I hate it, I fucking bloody well shagging HATE IT!

And here's another resident who doesn't seem all that keen on the place:

It's the geographical and spiritual home of "spice-boys" – steroid abusers with mullets who spend even more time over their hair than an American anchorwoman.

Swansea is the only place outside of Arkansas and Turkmenistan where having a mullet is considered cool.

Was once a town but within the last 30 years or so has got way above its station and become a small city. Swansea is the worst place in the world, in fact so bad is Swansea that Hell would fear being in the place. Car crime capital of Europe at one time, it's had that title stolen off it by Manchester, as the thieves in Swansea are actually too lazy to go out and steal a Vauxhall Belmont, Fiat Croma or Austin Montego. Two types of people live in Swansea: those who are too lazy to move elsewhere or those who are too poor to move.

The entire geographical area is full of arrogant pricks, fifty-something prostitutes, twats (for which read spice-boys, pikeys or charvers), arse-holes in tatty 318 or A4 cabriolets who drive down to Southend with the roof down but windows up (why?!), cheap sluts who drink in the local cheapo pub, drug addicts or those that aren't addicts are drug dealers, jobless dossers, people whose knuckles drag on the ground and village idiots – something Swansea excels at. It has several hundred idiots to each of its villages.

A posh night out in Swansea usually entails going to one of the Beefeater restaurants in the Marina or Mumbles or to one of the skanky holes in Mumbles where they think it's posh to bring the starter soup out on a tea-plate. So stupid are the local Council that they have released a television advert of Swansea to show people what it's like: A) all the places shown do NOT represent Swansea and B) they are showing it in the Swansea area. We already know what's in the city you fucktards.

The wettest place in the entire UK, coupled with the notes above, make Swansea the true shithole it is. Don't ever hold a door open for someone in Swansea because the entire 300K of people who live in the area will walk through the door without saying thank you or even nod. People are that arrogant in Swansea they would walk 15 miles just to go through a door you are holding open for them. A film called Twin Town was released a decade ago and if you want to know what Swansea is like then watch it without fear of visiting the place and being stabbed.

So, to summarise, Swansea, it's full of pricks and it's a real shitty city.

Hopefully you never experience Swansea, but if you ever visit the place then never leave your car or get off the train or bus. Best thing is to go straight past the place onto Llanelli, a pleasant place with a team that even let Motherwell beat them.

36

DRAFT MODERN MATHEMATICS PAPER 2009

HIGHLY CONFIDENTIAL

SWANSEA

Name . . . .
Nickname . . . .
Gangname . . . .

Steven the Stabber has bought half a kilo of cocaine for large. He wants to make 300% on the deal and still pay Mad Dai his 10% protection money. How much must he charge for a gram?

Tiny David reckons he'll get £42.50 extra Marriage Allowance a week if he ties the knot with Fat Alice. Even if he steals the ring, the wedding will cost him £587. And he'll have to start buying two fish and chips every night instead of one. How long will it be before David wishes he'd stayed single?

Joey and Billy stole a 2003 green Toyota 1600GL with 35,000 on the clock – and got a grand for it. How much more would they have got if it had been metallic silver, done 29,000 miles and had low profile tyres?

Jake the Flake and Fingers got grassed up for dealing speed. The Flake got 18 months but Fingers got three years. How many more previous convictions did Fingers have?

EXTRA CREDIT: Who was Fingers' brief?

37

TO BE SURE, TO BE SURE

Three men are sitting in the maternity ward of a hospital waiting for the imminent birth of their respective children. One is a Bluebird, one a Jack and the other a West Indian. They are all very nervous and pacing the floor – as you do in these situations.

Suddenly the doctor bursts through the double doors saying: "Gentlemen you won't believe this but your wives have all had their babies within five minutes of each other."

The men are beside themselves with happiness and joy.

"And," said the doctor, "They have all had little boys." The fathers are ecstatic and congratulate each other over and over.

"However, we do have one slight problem," the doctor said. "In all the confusion we may have mixed the babies up getting them to the nursery and would be grateful if you could join us there to try and help identify them."

With that the Bluebird raced past the doctor and bolted to the nursery. Once inside he picked up a dark skinned infant with tiny dreadlocks saying: "There's no doubt about it, this boy is mine!"

The doctor looked bewildered and said: "Well sir, of all the babies I would have thought that maybe this child could be of West Indian descent."

"That's a maybe," said the Bluebird, "but one of the other two is a Jack and I'm not taking the risk!"

38

FOOTBALL

The Post Office has just recalled their latest stamps. They had pictures of Swansea players on them and people couldn't work out which side to spit on.

And some Cardiff tunes:

When I was a little bitty boy,
My grandmother bought me a cute little toy,
Two Swansea fans, hanging on a string,
She told me to kick their fucking heads in.
Jacks on a string,
Jacks on a string,
She told me to kick their fucking heads in.
Jacks on a string,
Jacks on a string,
She told me to kick their fucking heads in.

If Football Teams Were Women:

Swansea – Sophie Ellis-Bextor
Individually all the components look fantastic – just doesn't work when put together.

Everton – Barbara Windsor

Been laughing at those tits so long we forget that once upon a time they actually looked quite good.

Fulham – Andrea Corr

Not bad to look at but not much of her. Seems a bit awestruck with fame.

Leicester City – Patsy Palmer

Generally a bit crap and second rate really, but some people like her.

Now make up your own.

39

YOU KNOW THAT YOU ARE LIVING IN A SWANSEA ESTATE WHEN

Your standard of living improves when you go camping.

Your neighbour has ever asked to borrow half a can of beer.

None of the tyres on your van are the same size.

You can get heroin delivered.

Your bin man is confused about what goes and what stays.

You actually wear shoes your dog brought home.

You've been in a punch-up at a jumble sale.

You carry a baseball bat in the front seat of your van so you can pacify the kids in the back.

40

CHAVS

Can often be found singing the Paul Allen ditty "The Mosh Song (Oi Mush)", a gentle piss-take of Jacks, by a Swansea Jack, of which this is the chorus:

I said "Oi Mush FUCK OFF who do you think you are
Don't you look at me like that. I'll do your fucking car"
I said "Oi Mush, FUCK OFF who do you think you are
Don't you look at me like that. I'll do your fucking car."

They usually can't do the verses, but it is worth checking out if you don't know it, as it is hilarious.

Chavs are the genital warts on the scrotum of society.

The Swansea Chav can be recognised in a number of ways:

1) The males will most certainly be wearing some form of tracksuit, probably Lacoste, with a not-so-matching pair of Rockport boots. The females, the Chavettes, usually delight in sporting the latest in

sunbed fashion ("A pound for forty five minutes? I'll 'ave a go,"), along with something revealing, such as a social security form tucked into their miniskirts.

2) A bloke with his hand down his crotch is a dead giveaway, as is a cap in any shape or form.

3) The females often sport a post-coital bump, usually uncovered, with a fag in one hand and their favourite bottle of peroxide in the other. How else do you explain year round bleach blond hair, with no sign of roots?

4) Chavlings (the spawn of adult Chavs) are usually recognised on the streets between 9 am and 3 pm weekdays, often riding a bicycle, which has usually been stolen. Their sole purpose is to follow in the footsteps of their mothers. The father is not usually known.

5) A good way to spot a chavette is that they wear earrings you could drive a bus through.

Legalised Chav Hunting:

We can advertise and promote to all would-be big game hunters. At £10,000 a bullet the Government could use the cash to subsidise the cost of the average Chav/Chavette seven child family, until through natural selection they themselves become the endangered species. Survival of the fittest would never become more relevant. How many Buckfast and cheap cider drinkers can outrun an open top Jeep with four overweight Americans equipped with sniper rifles and a highly-paid local guide?

Rules:

1. Anything in Kappa, Burberry, etc, is fair game.

2. See Rule 1.

Benefits:

Within two to four years large sections of Swansea would be open to all once more. JJB Sports, Sports Division, etc, would all close and Income and Council Tax will reduce.

Or possibly:

Far from being a blight on our communities a chav can both brighten our cities and educate our children, provided of course we have suitable containment. We would be able to surround them with high voltage enclosures such as those being used in our more modern jails. Visitors to the attraction would be able to see wild herds of the Common Chav hanging around at the base of authentically re-built housing blocks or trying to make rollies whilst swigging MD 20 20 at bus stops. Tours would be conducted in the shells of burnt-out police cars so as not to attract the attention of the chavs.

If, however, a tourist were approached by any of the chavs, the burnt-out police cars would be equipped with sound recordings of a school. This being the most alien of all sounds to a chav, he would be temporally confused and need a fix of spray solvent to help clear his mind.

There would be gift shops with shuttered windows and screens in front of the counters to enable young Cheeky Chavs to mingle with tourists and staff. Staff would be Working Chavs and heavily pregnant Chavettes, all trained to serve with an air of contempt for being made to do anything. Tourists and staff would have toilet facilities provided on every vertical concrete surface and any secluded passageways between shops or buildings.

Attached to the safari part of the attraction would be a fun park offering a full range of chav pastimes. The choices of activities would include: Driving around slowly listening to anything sub 20 hertz, allowing the squeaky whine of your Cruiser Chav guide to be heard above the pounding bass, and driving around quickly as above, but trying to throw all contraband out the window before the police catch up with you. If you were to favour more intellectual pursuits there would be daily games of *Who Wants To Be a Millionaire: The Benefits Edition* and *The Weakest Genetic Link*.

All patrons would receive lasting memories of their trip in the form of either a facial stab wound, severe tooth and gum disease, acute cholesterol problems or a photograph taken at the moment their first hit off the crack-pipe took effect.

And some chavlines:

Q. What is the difference between a dying chav and an onion?
A. Onions make you cry.

Q. Why are Chavs like slinkies?
A. They have no real use but it's great to watch one fall down a flight of stairs.

Q. What do you call a Chavette in a white tracksuit?
A. The bride.

Q. What's the difference between a Chav and a coconut?
A. One's thick and hairy, the other's a coconut.

Q. How do you get 100 Chavs into a phone box?
A. Paint three stripes on it.

Q. Two Chavs in a car without any music. Who's driving?
A. The police.

And of course there are the Jackcharvers, aka chavs, but specifically from Swansea.

Is that a dog turd over there or a Jack taking a rest?

Jack chavs are a government experiment which involved breeding rats and humans and has gone terribly wrong. Originally intended to create a type of drone army but instead created an ever-increasing group of city-dwelling smegma piles that live in tower blocks or boxes. It has recently been discovered that these genetically modified rats have little or no intelligence and only survive on basic instinct. Instead of fighting wars these vermin fight random people for "looking at them", will only fight one normal person at a time and there has to be at least 50

Jacks before any combat takes place. They also steal from old people, off licences and cars. Doesn't matter what it is, it could be a comb, they'll still have it.

General Jackcharver Image:

Jacks are often easy to spot as they hang around together and all look the same, whiteish (sometimes green), greasy, spotty, short haired, covered in "gold" jewellery (crafted by the finest £1 shop usually made from copper, tin plastic, etc). And of course the trackie bottoms, white sports socks, a woolly jumper/hooded over-throw jacket, baseball cap that teeters on the back of the head, white mucky trainers/fuck off pair of boots. They are unable to speak coherently.

Still, Jacks do maintain some sort of social/military structure. Be aware of the following invading your town:

Foot Jack Chav

Aged 13–16, they hang round outside off-licences, corners, and parks. Uniformed in the mandatory Adidas trackie bottoms tucked into white kappa sports socks. Any type of classic trainer:

Adidas/Reebok (Rockport boots worn for nights out). Weapons of choice: tin of spray paint, glass bottle.

Commander Jack Chav

Aged 17–20, requires a vehicle of some sort, usually a Vauxhall Nova, Astra, Ford Escort, Sierra, Suzuki 125 Trailblazer (used generally for snatching old ladies' handbags), all of which have been modified using scrap metal, Polyfilla, drainpipes and Lego. Dress code still the same as taste is not a quality found in any Jack. Weapon of choice: a baseball bat or a plank of wood located in the driver's side footwell, and "gold" knuckle-dusters.

General Jack Chav

There only can ever be one General Jack to each group of about 30 Jacks (6 Commanders, 18 Foot, 6 female Jackettes). A Jack leader is primitive looking, has to be over 25-years-old, have a criminal record which include any of these: burglary, theft, ABH, GBH and generally being offensive. Has to own a pair of jeans and a shirt, requires some sort of facial hair, has what may be classed as a human girlfriend, has to be a father, and has to have his own bedsit and sell drugs. In some cases addicted to heroin. Uniformed in a classic full all white Adidas tracksuit, Rockport boots nicely trimmed with the finest gold jewellery from Argos. Weapon of choice: an air rifle, piece of scaffolding, Alsatian or Rottweiler dog.

JACK QUESTIONS

What do you call a Jack in a box?
Innit.

What do you call a Jack in a filing cabinet?
Sorted.

What do you call a Jack on a bike?
A thief.

What do you call a Jack in a car?
Arrested.

What do you call a Jack in a bank?
A thief.

What do you call a Jack in a fridge?
Chillin'.

What do you call a Jack in a bus shelter?
At a party.

What do you call a 12-year-old Jack girl?
Pregnant.

What do you call a Jack girl without any children?
Under the age of 10.

Why did the Jack cross the road?
To punch someone for no reason.

What's a Jack's favourite car?
One without an alarm.

What do you call a Jack in a coffin?
A damn good reason to kill another.

What do you call two dead Jacks?
A good start to the day.

What do Jacks use as protection during sex?
A bus shelter.

What do you say to a Jack with a job?
Can I have a Big Mac please?

What's the difference between a dead fox and a dead Jack in the road?
  The dead fox has skid marks in front of it.

What do you call a 30-year-old Jackette?
Dunno, ask her 17-year-old son.

What do you do if you run a Jack over?
Slip it into reverse just to make sure.

Sign on the roadside near a Swansea hospital: Hospital Quiet Zone. Please Use Silencers On Your Shooters.

Sticker on a Swansea car:
Toot if you love peace and quiet.

Another sticker on a chav car:
Pardon my driving, I am reloading.

41

CARDIFF BANTER

Grow your own dope. Plant a Jack.

Q. What's the first question at a Swansea pub quiz?
   A. What are you looking at?

Q. Why does the River Tawe run through Swansea?
   A. Because if it walked it would be mugged.

Q. What do you call a Jack in a three-bedroom semi?
   A. A burglar.

To a theatre audience:

"Have you all switched off your mobile phones? And have the people from Swansea turned off their electronic tags?"

Jacks consider themselves well dressed if their socks match.

42

HOW TO HANDLE STRESS

Picture yourself near a stream.

Birds are softly chirping in the crisp, cool mountain air.

Nothing can bother you here. No one knows this secret place.

You are in total seclusion from that place called "the world".

The soothing sound of a gentle waterfall fills the air with a cascade of serenity.

The water is clear. You can easily make out the face of the Swansea person whose head you're holding under the water.

There now . . . feeling better?

43

ADVICE AND CONTROVERSY

A Jack goes to his doctor to find out what's wrong with him.

"Your problem is that you are fat," says the doctor.

"I'd like a second opinion," responds the man.

"Okay," replies the doctor, "you are ugly too."

Oooh, Controversial:

Description of the election process in Cardiff: "Poli", in Latin meaning "many", and "tics" meaning "blood-sucking creatures".

Warning:

"He needed killin'," is a valid defence in Swansea courts.

The top 10 things not to say to a Jack cop when you get stopped for speeding:

I can't reach my licence unless you hold my Buckfast.

Sorry officer, I didn't realize my radar detector wasn't plugged in.

You must have been doing 125 to keep up with me, excellent driving.

I thought you had to be in relatively good physical shape to be a police officer.

You're not going to check the boot, are you?

I pay your wages, boyo.

Great, officer, that's terrific. The last monkey only gave me a warning as well.

I was trying to keep up with traffic. Yes, I know there are no other cars about, that's how far they are ahead of me.

Well, when I reached down to pick up my bag of crack, my shotgun fell off my lap and got stuck between the brake and the accelerator, forcing me to speed.

What do you mean 'have I been drinking'? You're the trained specialist.

44

SCHOOL TALES, TALL AND TRUE

Somewhere in darkest Swansea, an Attendance Officer accompanied by a Deputy Head (safety in numbers) went into a block of flats to speak to a family about the daughter's poor attendance.

As they climbed the stairs they spotted a large Rottweiler patrolling the landing outside the flat they were going to visit. Undaunted by this slavering beast, they rang the bell. The door was opened and in rushed the dog. They were greeted by the mother and taken into the barely furnished living room.

The conversation wasn't going too well and to make matters worse, the DHT saw the dog cock its leg and pee up against a wall in the room. Nobody said anything and he decided to keep quiet.

The conversation became more heated and then he saw the dog do a shit in the corner. Again nobody mentioned it.

Eventually, the Attendance Officer decided to call a halt to the meeting as the family were becomingly increasingly hostile towards their callers.

They were shown out somewhat abruptly and started to walk downstairs, both glad to have escaped, when the flat door was thrown open and the father shouted after them:

"An' you can take your fucking dog with you!"

One day a boy went into his Classics class and placed a lump of rock on his teacher's desk. When the teacher asked where this rock had come from, the pupil replied: "It's a present from my big brother (a former pupil). He was in Greece with the army and he chipped a bit off the Parthenon for you."

These immortal words were heard during a typical heated class discussion:

"You've got a face like a second-hand dartboard."

In a recent written Home Economics test in Swansea on cookery, the pupils were asked to write down the names of three typical Jack dishes.

One pupil carefully wrote: "A plate, a cup and a saucer."

45

DOGGED SUPER SALESMAN

When the shop manager of a large Cardiff tailor's returned from lunch, he noticed that the sales assistant's hand was bandaged, but before he could ask about the bandage the guy said he had some very good news for him.

"Guess what?" he said. "I finally sold that terrible suit we've had on the rack for so long."

"Do you mean that repulsive pink-and-orange double-breasted monstrosity?" the manager asked.

"The very one."

"That's brilliant," the manager cried, "I thought we'd never get rid of that horrible thing. That had to be the ugliest suit we've ever had. But why is your hand bandaged?"

The salesman replied: "It was David Blunkett that bought it, and his guide dog bit me."

46

ANOTHER GOOD DOG

Four men were boasting about how clever their dogs were. The first man was an engineer, the second man was an accountant, the third man was a chemist and the fourth was from Swansea.

To show off, the engineer said to his dog: "Protractor, do your trick." Protractor trotted over to a desk, took out some paper and a pen, and promptly drew a circle, a square, and a triangle.

Everyone agreed that was pretty clever. However, the accountant said his dog could do better. He called his dog and said: "Slide Rule, do your trick." Slide Rule went into the kitchen, returned with a dozen biscuits and divided them into four equal piles of three each.

Everyone agreed that was pretty good, but the chemist said his dog could do better. He called his dog and said: "Measure, do your trick." Measure got up, walked to the fridge in the kitchen, took out a pint of milk, got a glass from the cupboard and poured exactly a half pint without spilling a drop.

Everyone agreed that was good. The three men turned to the Jack and said, "What can your dog do?" He called to his dog and said: "Catkiller, do your trick." Catkiller jumped to his feet, ate the biscuits, drank the milk, peed on the paper, sexually assaulted the other three dogs, claimed he injured his back while doing so, filed a complaint about unsafe working conditions, put in for compen and went home on the Pat and Mick.

JUST ANOTHER DAY IN SWANSEA

It rained and rained and rained and rained,

The average was well maintained,

And when our fields were simply bogs,

It started raining cats and dogs.

After a drought of half an hour,

There came a most refreshing shower,

And then the queerest thing of all,

A gentle rain began to fall.

Next day 'twas pretty fairly dry,

Save for a deluge from the sky.

This wetted people to the skin,

But after that the rain set in.

We wondered what's the next we'd get,

As sure as fate we got more wet,

But soon we'll have a change again,

And we shall have,

A drop of rain!

48

AND FINALLY, LAST CALL

It was Jack Pat's last day on the job after 35 years of carrying the post through all kinds of weather to the same neighbourhoods of Cardiff. Everybody knew Jack Pat, though they didn't of course speak to him much.

But surprise! When he arrived at the first house, he was greeted by the whole family there, who all hugged and congratulated him and sent him on his way with a cheque for £50.

At the second house they presented him with superb Cuban cigars in an 18-carat gold box, while the folk at the third house gave him a case of 30-year-old Scotch.

At the fourth house he was met at the door by a stunning blonde in her lingerie. She took him by the arm and led him up the stairs to the bedroom where she blew his mind with the most passionate love he had ever experienced.

When he had had enough they went downstairs, where the woman made him a giant breakfast: eggs, tomatoes, bacon, sausage, beans, black pudding, the complete heart-stopper, and freshly-squeezed orange juice. When he was truly satisfied she poured him a cup of steaming coffee. As she was pouring, he noticed a five pound note sticking out from under the cup's bottom edge.

"All this was just too wonderful for words," he said, "but what's the fiver for?"

"Well," said the blonde, "last night, I told my husband that today would be your last day, and that we should do something special for you. I asked him what to give you. He said: 'Fuck him. Give him a fiver.' The breakfast was my idea."

JACKS

VS.

BLUEBIRDS

JACKS START HERE

First published 2009
by Black & White Publishing Ltd
29 Ocean Drive, Edinburgh EH6 6JL

1 3 5 7 9 10 8 6 4 2   09 10 11 12 13

ISBN: 978 1 84502 281 5

Text © Ian Black 2009

The right of Ian Black to be identified as the author of this work has
been asserted by him in accordance with the Copyright, Designs and
Patents Act 1988.

All rights reserved. No part of this publication may be reproduced,
stored in a retrieval system, or transmitted in any form, or by any
means, electronic, mechanical, photocopying, recording or otherwise,
without permission in writing from the publisher.

A CIP catalogue record for this book is available from the British Library.

Typeset by RefineCatch Limited, Bungay, Suffolk
Printed and bound by CPI Cox & Wyman, Reading

INTRODUCTION

Just to give you the flavour of how much Jacks and Bluebirds mutually detest each other, try this little jibe from the Swansea terraces: Thieves broke into the trophy room of Legoland, as the Swans have lovingly christened Cardiff's Stadium, and stole the entire contents. Police are looking for a big carpet.

Or how about a song?

The Cardiff train came over the hill,
And she blew, she blew,
The Cardiff train came over the hill,
And she blew, she blew,
The Cardiff train came over the hill,
The brakes they failed and they all got killed.
AAAAAAHHHH!

In a survey of UK football fans, Cardiff fans have proved to be the most likely to have had sex in the shower. In the survey, carried out for a leading toiletries firm, 86 percent of Cardiff fans said that they have enjoyed sex in the shower.

The other 14 percent said they hadn't even been to prison yet.

Or how about: A Bluebird is leaving the ground after yet another tactical disaster. A prostitute comes up to him and says: "Do you fancy a blow job?" He stares at her in that dim, Bluebird-like way, and asks: "Will it affect my Giro?"

There is a much quoted Swansea slogan for Cardiff: "A castle, a smile and a song . . . one out of three isn't bad."

And of course traditionally there is no request to tea in Cardiff, more of a statement, delivered without the question mark, as in: "You'll have had your tea." These days, instead of the offer of a drink it is: "You'll be driving."

As for the sheepshagging stories about the Swans, everybody in Swansea knows that in Cardiff it is male sheep that get shagged, and not just in the Masonic lodges. And they couldn't tell an ugly sheep from a pretty one anyway.

One Swansea woman summed up her feelings succinctly: "I wouldn't want to move to a place where you have to put on matching clothing to pick up the milk from the doorstep."

Cardiffians, or Scumdiffians from Caaardeff equate breeding with good form, whereas in Swansea they accept it as good fun.

There is a fairly prevalent paranoid myth among Bluebirds that all Jacks want to move to

Cardiff and drive down property values, just out of badness.

The people of the two cities have traditionally always regarded each other with the greatest possible loathing, mistrust and contempt. They are both absolutely right. This book is the proof.

These are hard hits and sneaky bits from the Swansea side, sharp jibes and bludgeoning diatribes, but it's just friendly rivalry really. To use the double positive negative, a figure of speech used in both cities: "Aye, right."

1

ATTITUDES AND INSULTS

A quote from an economist who wishes to remain unidentified in case he becomes unidentified remains: "Swansea is still transfixed by its days of industrial and shipbuilding glory in the 19th and 20th centuries. Cardiff is doing quite well in the 18th."

The standard disparagement of: "Fur coat and no knickers," that is applied by the Jack to the Bluebird to illustrate the pretension to gentility so despised in Swansea is turned on its head by this tale of two girls going for a night out. One is from Swansea, one is from Cardiff.

Cardiff girl says, "Hang on a minute, I'll have to put on my knickers."

Swansea girl looks shocked and says, "Knickers! On a night out?"

Another Swansea phrase that sums this up:
Curtains at the window and no sheets on the bed.

A Bluebird, finally roused by a Jack's needling, protested that he was born a Bluebird and hoped to die an Bluebird.

"Christ Almighty," said the Swan, "have you no ambition at all?"

Jacks travel to Cardiff, Bluebirds make expeditions to Swansea. And they are not tense while in Swansea, just terribly, terribly alert.

Said by a Swansea man of a hypocritical Cardiff man when informed of his demise, "No doubt he'll get into heaven, but God won't like him. And it will be mutual."

You get more laughs at a Swansea funeral than at a wedding in Cardiff.

What's the difference between a Butetown man and a large pizza?

A large pizza can feed a family of four.

In Cardiff, about the only concession to gaiety is a striped shroud.

A Swansea Jack and a Bluebird girl are in a bar when the girl notices something strange about the wellies that the guy's wearing.

She says to him, "Excuse me, but why does one of your wellies have an L on it, and the other one's got an R on it?"

The Jack smiles, puts down his pint of Boggles Trout Piss and replies, "Well, I am a little bit dense, you see. The one with the R is for my right foot and the one with the L is for my left foot."

"Right'!" exclaims the girl, "So THAT'S why my knickers have got C&A on them."

A Swansea woman driver is pulled over by a policeman on the way out of Cardiff.

"Is there a problem, officer?"

"Yes, madam, you were speeding."

"Really?"

"May I see your licence please?"

"I'd give it to you but I don't have one."

"Don't have one?"

"No. Lost it after drunk driving four times."

"I see . . . May I see your vehicle registration papers please?"

"No. Can't do that either."

"Why not?"

"Well . . . I stole this car."

"Stole it?"

"Yes, after I killed and chopped up the owner."

"You what?"

"Lost my temper. It was messy. His body is in a pile of plastic bags in the boot if you want to see."

The policeman looks at the woman for a second, then backs away to his car and calls for reinforcements. Within minutes there are more police cars circling them. A police sergeant approaches the car.

He clears his throat, then calls to her, "Madam, please step out of and away from your vehicle."

She does so. "Is there a problem, sir?"

"One of my officers told me that you have stolen this car and murdered the owner."

"Murdered the owner?"

"Yes. Could you open the boot of your car please?"

She does, and they both look down into a dusty, empty space.

"Is this your car, madam?"

"Yes. Here are the registration papers."

The sergeant scans through them and sees that they are in order.

"My officer claims that you do not have a driving licence."

The woman rummages through her bag then hands her licence to the puzzled sergeant.

"Mrs Smith, my officer told me you didn't have a licence, that you stole this car, and that you murdered and dismembered the owner."

"I'll bet the lying Bluebird bastard told you I was speeding too!"

A young Bluebird stockbroker makes a ton of dough from a somewhat dodgy deal and celebrates not being caught by going out and buying a brand new Ferrari 550. He takes it out for a spin and, intoxicated by the speed and handling, is nearly in Swansea before he looks out and notices where he is. Panicking slightly when he discovers that he has to get off the motorway in Swanland to turn, he nevertheless does and is stopped at a red traffic light.

An old Jack on a moped pulls up next to him. The old man looks over the sleek, shiny car and asks, "What kind of motor have you got there, son?"

The young man replies, "A Ferrari 550 – it cost 100 grand."

"That's a lot of cash," says the old man. "Why did it cost so much?"

"Because this car can do up to 220 miles an hour!" he says proudly.

The moped driver asks, "Mind if I take a look inside?"

"No problem, just try not to breathe on the upholstery," replies the owner. So the old man pokes his head in the window and looks around.

Then sitting back on his moped, the old man says, "That's a pretty nice car, you've got there, but I think I'll stick with my moped. I've seen the day, though, when I would have given you a race."

Just then, the light changes to green so the guy decides to show the old man just what his car can do.

He shouts: "Right, you Jack coffin-dodger," floors it, and within 15 seconds the speedometer reads 160 mph.

Suddenly, he notices a dot in his rear view mirror. It seems to be getting closer.

He slows down to see what it could be and suddenly, whoooooooosssshhhh! Something whips past him, going much faster.

"What could be going faster than my flying machine?" the young man asks himself.

He floors the accelerator again and takes the Ferrari up to 200 mph. then, up ahead of him, he sees that it is the old man on the moped.

Amazed that the moped could pass his Ferrari and just a little bit apprehensive about the insult, he gives it some more welly and passes the moped at 210 mph.

Whhhhooooooosssssshhhh!!! He's feeling pretty good until he looks in his mirror and sees the old man gaining on him again.

Astounded by the speed of this old guy he floors the accelerator and takes the Ferrari all the way up to 220 mph. Not ten seconds later, he sees the moped bearing down on him again. The Ferrari is flat out and there's nothing he can do. He is shitting bricks by now, as he thinks that the Jack is out for revenge.

Suddenly, the moped ploughs into the back of his Ferrari, demolishing the rear end. He skids to a halt as the car catches fire. The young man jumps out, wishing he'd insured it, and unbelievably, the old man is still alive.

He runs up to the mangled old guy and says, "Oh my God! Is there anything I can do for you?"

The old man says . . .

"Before I burn to death, please unhook my fucking braces from your wing mirror!"

Swansea's kids are not better natural fighters than Cardiff kids. They are just better trained and have better weaponry.

How many Bluebird graduates does it take to screw in a light bulb?

One; he stands still and the world revolves around him.

Tom the Swan is up in court in Swansea, after running down two Bluebirds with his car.

The judge says: "Now we have heard the evidence given, have you anything to say before I pass sentence?"

"Well," Tom says, "I had been out for a drive and I was making my way home, doing 30 mph, minding the speed limit, when out from between two cars stepped these two people, and I hit them. One came through the windscreen, the other went over the hedge."

The judge looks at Tom and says: "We have all heard the eyewitness reports, would you like to try again and tell the court what happened?"

"Ok," says Tom. "Well, I was trying to get home for my tea, the traffic had been bad, got to an open bit of road, I might have been doing about 45 mph in the 30 zone, when these two poofy-looking guys stepped out in front of me and I hit them. One came through the windscreen the other went over the hedge."

"Getting a bit more like the evidence now," says the judge, "Would you like one more chance?"

"Oh God, ok," says Tom. "Right, I'd been at the Swansea/Cardiff game and the bastards beat us three

nil. I was pissed off, so I was belting along at 75 mph to get to the pub to drown my sorrows, when I see these two Cardiff fans walking along the road in their poncy fifty quid shirts. So I think, right you bastards, mounted the pavement, chased them for a bit, then got the twats. One came through the windscreen and the other went over the hedge."

"That's better," said the judge "It's now my duty to pass sentence. We'll charge one with breaking and entering, and the other for leaving the scene of the crime."

In Cardiff a dog can teach a boy many things – fidelity, perseverance, and to turn around three times before lying down.

What do you sing to a Bluebird taking a bath?
  Happy Birthday To You.

A Bluebird has all the qualities of a poker, except its occasional warmth.

What's the difference between Bluebirds and a jet engine?
  A jet engine eventually stops whining.

What are the two worst things about a Bluebird?

His (or her) face.

What they drink in Cardiff a lot is advocaat, which sounds, looks and tastes like it has been distilled from the juice of the backbones of lawyers.

The phone rang in a Cardiff pub and the landlord answered it.

"This is the IRA," the voice said. "There's a bomb in your pub and you've got five minutes to get out."

The owner put the phone down and went back to the bar.

"Last orders, everyone!" he shouted.

A Jack walks into a bar and says, "Give me a triple vodka!" He quickly downs it and says, "Another!" Again he sinks it and demands, "Another!"

He keeps on drinking until, after his eighth, the barman says, "Hey, you drink like you've got a problem. Do you want to talk about it?"

The guy says, "Ten years I've been with my wife, even though she's a Bluebird. I left work early today, to surprise her. I came home to find her in bed with my best friend."

"What did you say to them?" asks the barman.

"I told her to get back to Cardiff, and I told him 'Bad dog, bad dog!' "

The Jack was through in Cardiff for the night and was having a quiet pint. A live band filed in to the pub and started to play a selection of Bluebird songs.

As tune followed tune, all in praise of the far from mighty City, he leaned over the bar and shouted in the barman's ear: "Is it just all Bluebird songs or does this band play anything on request?"

"Oh yes, they do," said the barman.

"That's great," said the Jack. "Ask them to go outside and play hopscotch."

2

SIGNS

You've been in Cardiff too long when:

You think Jacks are unsavoury, but you've never met any as you are too scared to go to Swansea after dark in case somebody steals one of your eleven mobile phones.

You think it is your God-given right to slag all the other places in Wales.

You think paying £10 for a three minute cab ride is perfectly acceptable.

You will sulk at the champagne being warm at Christmas.

You sulk if there are no after-club parties because you can't possibly go to bed before 11.30 am the next day.

You will sulk if you don't manage to spend £1000 on your credit card in your lunch hour.

You are working for the Government in Cardiff:

When someone asks about what you do for a living, you lie.

You get really excited about a two percent pay raise.

Your biggest loss from a system crash is that you lose your best jokes.

Your supervisor doesn't have the ability to do your job.

You sit in a cubicle smaller than your bedroom cupboard.

Computer specialists know less about computers than your teenager.

Lunch is like another scheduled meeting, but shorter.

If you see a good looking person you know he or she is a visitor.

Management thinks a business trip with uncompensated mandatory weekend travel is a perk.

Although you have a telephone, pager, E-mail, FAX, company distribution, mail and co-workers sitting right on the other side of the partition . . . communication is a continuing problem.

You know, and everyone who works with you knows, that your performance is superior, but "satisfactory" is the highest level on the documented performance rating.

You work 200 hours for the £100 bonus and jubilantly say, "Oh great, thanks very much!"

When workers screw up they are transferred to

another office to be someone else's problem; when management screws up they are promoted.

Your boss's favourite lines are "when you get a few minutes," "in your spare time," "when you're free" and "I have an opportunity for you."

Training is something spoken about but never seen.

A holiday is something you'll get next year . . . maybe.

The worst possible reputation comes from being the initiator of a complaint.

3

CARDIFF Q & A

Q: What do you call a Cardiff man with a sheep under one arm and a goat under the other?
A: Bisexual.

Q: What do Bluebirds use as a form of contraception?
A: Their personalities.

Q: What do you do if you see a Bluebird with half a face?
A: Stop laughing and reload!

Q: What do you say to a Bluebird with money?
A: Anything you like, he's not listening . . . and, if he inherited it, he can't even see you.

Q: What do you do when you see an endangered animal that is eating an endangered plant in Cardiff?
A: Make sure that you don't make eye contact with anyone.

4

THE CARDIFF CHRISTMAS CAROL

Late last week, I was rushing around trying to get some last minute shopping done. I was stressed out and not thinking very fondly of the Festive season right then. It was dark, cold, and wet as I was loading my car with gifts that I felt obligated to buy. I noticed that I was missing a receipt that I might need later. So, mumbling under my breath, I retraced my steps to the shop entrance.

As I was searching the wet pavement for the lost receipt, I heard a quiet sobbing. The crying was coming from a poorly dressed boy of about 12-years-old. He was short and thin. He had no coat and was just wearing a ragged flannel shirt to protect him from the cold night's chill.

Oddly enough, he was holding a hundred pound note in his hand. Thinking that he had become separated from his parents in the busy shop, I asked him what was wrong. He told me his sad story. He said that he came from a large family. He had three brothers and four sisters. His father had died when he was nine-years-old. His mother was poorly

educated and worked at two full time jobs. She made very little to support her large family.

Nevertheless, she had managed to skimp and save £200 to buy her children Christmas presents. The young boy had been dropped off, by his mother, on the way to her second job. He was to use the money to buy presents for all his siblings and save just enough to take the bus home. He had not even entered the shop when an older boy grabbed one of the hundred pound notes and disappeared into the night.

"Why didn't you scream for help?" I asked.

The boy said, "I did."

"And nobody came to help you?" I wondered.

The boy stared at the pavement and sadly shook his head.

"How loud did you scream?" I inquired.

The soft-spoken boy looked up and meekly whispered, "Help me!"

I realised that absolutely no one could have heard that boy cry for help.

So I grabbed his other hundred and ran to the car.

5

TRUE TALES

A Jack designer, who has designs on moving to Cardiff and wishes to remain anonymous (easy, peasy lemon squeezy in Cardiff, one would think) claims that Cardiff women wear: "Clothing that looks as if it was designed and made by people who had had clothes described to them, but who had never seen any."

Two Bluebird ladies had been enticed to Swansea for the sales and were resting their barking dogs in a tearoom, having spent two hours looking for the cheapest one. One said to the friendly waitress who asked what they wanted: "None of your Swansea banter, thanks, just tea, and I hope my cup is clean."

The waitress bustled off and returned with a pot of tea a moment or so later, asking cheerily: "Which one of you wanted the clean cup?"

The *Evening News* sent a reporter to interview the oldest man in Cardiff, Dai Snoddie.

"And exactly how old are you, Mr Snoddie?" asked the young reporter.

"One-hundred-and-three-years-old today, son," croaked Snoddie.

"And I'm sure you've seen a fair few changes in your time, sir."

"I have indeed, son. And I've been against them all."

A young Jack couple went to visit an estate agent in Cardiff.

"Right," said the agent. "Just tell me your starting price, then we'll all have good laugh and take it from there."

In Cardiff, if a mute swears, his mother washes his hands with soap. In Swansea they just give him the finger.

Cardiff folk are so narrow-minded that even when they get an idea it comes out neatly folded.

Cardiff, where no shirt is too young to be stuffed.

Man walking along a road in the countryside comes across a shepherd and a huge flock of sheep. Tells

the shepherd, "I will bet you £100 against one of your sheep that I can tell you the exact number in this flock."

The shepherd thinks it over; it's a big flock, so he takes the bet.

"973," says the man. The shepherd is astonished, because that is exactly right.

Says "OK, I'm a man of my word, take an animal." The man picks one up and begins to walk away.

"Wait," cries the shepherd, "Let me have a chance to get even. Double or nothing that I can guess your exact occupation." The man says okay.

"You are an economist for the Home Office in Cardiff," says the shepherd.

"Amazing!" responds the man, "You are exactly right! But tell me, how did you deduce that?"

"Well," says the shepherd, "put down my dog and I'll tell you."

Cardiff estate dwellers love cats. They taste just like chicken.

"You seem to have more than the average share of intelligence for a man of your background," said the Bluebird advocate to a Jack witness.

"If I wasn't under oath, I'd return the compliment," replied the witness

Two Bluebirds boarded a flight. One sat in the window seat, the other sat in the middle seat. Just before takeoff, a Jack got on and took the aisle seat next to the two Bluebirds.

The Jack kicked off his shoes, wiggled his toes and was settling in when the guy in the window seat said: "I think I'll get up and get a beer."

"No problem," said the Jack, "I'll get it for you."

While he was gone, one of the Bluebirds picked up the Jack's shoe and spat in it.

When he returned with the beer, the other guy said, "That looks good, I think I'll have one too."

Again, the Jack obligingly went to fetch it and while he was gone, the other guy picked up the other shoe and spat in it.

The Jack returned and they all sat back and enjoyed the flight. As the plane was landing, the Jack slipped his feet into his shoes and knew immediately what had happened.

He turned to them and asked passionately, "How long must this go on? This fighting between our cities? This hatred? This animosity? This spitting in shoes and pissing in beers?"

Bluebird paedophile: "You'll have had your sweetie."

Even cheaper Bluebird paedophile: "Do you want to buy a sweet?"

"What's this diet you're doing?" asked the Bluebird of the Jack.

"It's called the booze diet, I've lost three days already."

Swansea recipe: Take a pound. Buy chips. Put salt and vinegar on them. Eat them.

Cardiff recipe: Take a pound. Buy chips. Pretend you made them. Eat them.

Swansea saying: As cheap as chips.

Cardiff saying: As dear as chips.

Two prisoners are talking about their crimes:

George: "I robbed a bank, and they gave me 20 years."

Jim: "Hmm. I killed a man, and I'm here for three days."

George: "What? I rob a bank and get 20 years; you kill a man and get three days?"

Jim: "Well, it was a Cardiff lawyer."

Bluebirds are even allowed to travel the world and this year one was reported as being the only survivor

of a plane crash when a jumbo went down in the South China Sea. The man was found clinging to a piece of board the size of a fag packet but had not been touched by the sharks which had quickly snapped up his fellow passengers.

The Mate of the rescue ship was a Jack and when the Australian skipper of the rescue vessel expressed astonishment at the survival of the Cardiff man he pointed to the dripping exhausted man lying flat on his back on the deck and said: "See that t-shirt? It says 'Cardiff for the Premier league title'. Not even a shark is going to swallow that."

Bluebirds comb their hair in order to make an impression on the pillow.

A Bluebird, an Irishman, a Jack and a Tory MP were sharing a railway carriage.

The MP was reading the Daily Mail, and after a time he sighed with exasperation, screwed his paper up into a ball and threw it into the waste basket.

The other passengers were shocked and asked why he had done that.

He said: "Well, in this country, opinions like those are ten a penny."

The Bluebird was drinking a whisky he had

brought from the bar when a similar mood of exasperation seemed to descend on him and he threw the glass in the bin.

"Why did you do that?" asked the others.

"Well, in my salary bracket, whiskies like that are ten a penny."

The journey continued and the Irishman began to get restless and flung his book to join the other discards.

"Before you ask," he said, "in my part of the world authors are ten a penny."

The Jack had been sitting quietly when he suddenly lunged forward, pinioned the Bluebird and stuffed him headfirst into the bin.

"Why did you do that?" they asked him.

He said: "Felt like it."

People in Cardiff equate breeding with good form, whereas in Swansea they accept it as good fun.

Cardiff ladies say things like: "Oh Janet, he was just a bit too friendly . . . a real Jack. He came up to me on the bus and put his hand up my skirt . . . you know the Jaeger one with the pleats."

Swansea has been described as savagely egalitarian, Cardiff as civilly fascist.

A Jack family are on a trip to rellies in Cardiff. On the way back into town on the bus they find themselves behind a fur-coated lady, whose eyes rake them disapprovingly as she sits down with an almost audible sniff. The youngest child has one of those enormous drippy lollipops and is eventually wiping the drips off on the lady's collar.

The Jack mum notes the lady's discomfort, just as she had noted the disapproval earlier, and says: "Jasmine, stop that!"

She then waits till she sees the lady relax a fraction before continuing: "You'll get your lolly all hairy."

The two Bluebird school inspectors were in an estate in Swansea waiting for a taxi, having been silly enough to leave their car outside the school. They noticed a Fort Knox of a pub and took note of the rough hand-lettered sign on the door, which read: "We have plain drinks and we have fancy drinks."

Reading this, the two Bluebirds smirked at each other and went in, scuffing their feet through the sawdust on the floor.

"Last night's furniture," said one, grinning condescendingly.

There was a barman with his back to them washing glasses, so they started talking.

One of them, addressing space, said: "Seeing that they serve fancy drinks here, I'll have a gin rickey, maybe with a smoked olive. What are you going to have?" he added, addressing his fellow would-be joker.

"Good choice," said the other, "I think I'll try a dry martini cocktail, made with French vermouth, and a spiced cocktail onion, one of the coloured ones. Pink, perhaps."

Without shifting his position or lifting his eyes from his work the barman said: "I can kick the arse of any given two Bluebird space-wasters in 11.2 seconds. That's my record, but I know I can beat it with you two. And I haven't even turned round yet."

6

STUPID BLUEBIRDS

The Jack and the Bluebird were on a parachute training course. The Bluebird jumped first, pulled the rip-cord and started to float down. The Jack followed, but when he pulled his cord, nothing happened. When he pulled the emergency cord, again nothing happened.

As the Jack plummeted past, the Bluebird shouted, "So we're in a race are we?" and ripped off his parachute.

After pulling a Jack over for speeding, a member of Cardiff's finest started to lecture him about his speed, pompously implying that the Jack didn't know any better and trying to make him feel as uncomfortable as possible. He finally started writing out the ticket, but had to keep swatting at some flies buzzing around his head.

The Jack asked, "Having some problems with circle flies there, are you?"

The policeman paused to take another swipe and said, "Well, yes, if that's what they are. I've never heard of circle flies."

The Jack was pleased to enlighten the cop. "Circle flies are most common on farms. They're called circle flies because you almost always find them circling the backside of a horse."

The policeman continues writing for a moment, then says, "Are you trying to call me a horse's arse?"

"Oh no, officer," the farmer replies. "I have too much respect for your particular force and police officers for that."

"Good job," the cop says snidely, then goes back to writing him up.

After a long pause the Jack added, "Hard to fool those flies, though."

In Cardiff everyone can do one thing better than everybody else. It's usually reading their own hand-writing on the confession.

You can always tell a Bluebird, but you can't tell him much.

This Bluebird walks into a book shop. He asks the clerk, "Can I have a play by Shakespeare?"

The assistant says, "Of course, sir. Which one?"

The Bluebird says, "William."

Jack tourist: "This seems like a very dangerous cliff. It's a wonder they don't put up a warning sign."

Bluebird: "Yes, it is dangerous, but they kept a warning sign up for two years and no one fell over, so it was taken down."

How do you know when a Bluebird is about to say something intelligent?

When he starts his sentence with, "A Jack once told me . . ."

How to Describe a Dumb Bluebird:

He's got the full six-pack, but not the plastic thingy to hold it all together.

A gross ignoramus: 144 times worse than an ordinary ignoramus.

He's an ignoranus – an ignorant arsehole.

He's got a photographic memory, but no lens.

He donated his brain to science before he was finished using it.

He fell out of his family tree.

The gates are shut, the lights are flashing, but the train isn't coming.

He has two brains; one is lost and the other is out looking for it.

If brains were taxed, he'd get a rebate.

7

JACK PHILOSOPHY

Welsh by birth; British by law; Jack by the grace of God.

The war between Swansea and Cardiff will not determine who is right – only who is left. And it won't start with C.

Swansea saying: No man is an island, except in his bath.

As they say in Swansea: "Dear God, grant me patience, but get a move on, man!"

A Bluebird is a man who feels badly when he feels good for fear he'll feel worse when he feels better.

Showing-off is a hanging offence in Cardiff.

How many Bluebirds does it take to change a light bulb?

None, they form a self help group called: "How to cope with life in the dark."

Swansea saying: Life is shite. Get a fucking helmet, okay?

To the Scotsman, the glass is half full.

To the Englishman, the glass is half empty.

To the Bluebird, the glass is twice as big as it needs to be.

Cardiff is so middle class and middle of the road it should be called White Line City. It would also make it cosier-sounding and more like home for the junkies.

In Cardiff they say: "If at first you don't succeed, redefine success."

In Swansea they say: "If at first you don't succeed, ah, fuck it."

There are two golden rules for life in Swansea:

1) Never tell people everything.

It is truly said (by a Jack) that if all of the editions of all of the books about Harry Potter were laid end to end, it would still be raining in Cardiff.

Incidentally, it is a little known fact that the best-selling author of the above has been known to take a drink. You can tell from her name, Jakey Rowling.

In Cardiff a true friend will pay the bail to get you out of jail. In Swansea a true friend will be sitting beside you in jail saying: "We fucked that up, bach."

One of the Jack pastimes is to visit Cardiff to play a game called Spot the Jack. If you spot one you win and can go home immediately. Nobody has ever won.

Cardiff's public schools are often blamed, probably because it is their fault, for the stiffness and emotional coldness which has led Jacks to dub Bluebirds "God's frozen people".

Casual Swansea acceptance of immigrants: "Wonder what their chips will be like."

In Cardiff there is a comfortable time-lag of a century or so intervening between the perception

that something ought to be done and a serious attempt to do it.

In Cardiff real friends help you move. In Swansea real friends help you move bodies.

Bluebird: "Hard work pays off in the future."
  Jack: "Laziness pays off now."

Swansea saying: The Cardiff gene pool would be none the worse of a little chlorine.

Swansea saying: He who laughs last thinks slowest.

In Cardiff, a penny saved is a penny earned. In Swansea, a penny saved is just stupid. What can you buy with a penny?

Jack to Bluebird: I've seen better looking faces on pirate flags.

Swansea saying: Ambition is a poor excuse for not having enough sense to be lazy.

In Cardiff they say: "Don't force it, be careful."
  In Swansea they say: "Get a bigger hammer."

Cardiff! Too many freaks, not enough circuses.

Cardiff's suburbia: where they tear up the trees & then name streets after them.

Jack threat to Bluebird: You! Off my planet!

Nothing is ever a complete failure; it can always serve as a bad example. Look at Cardiff.

Swansea High Court Judge: "You are charged with throwing the Bluebird out of the third floor window."

Jimmy: "It was my Jack temper. I did it without thinking."

Judge: "Yes, I understand that, but don't you see how dangerous it might have been for anyone on the street below?"

"I have a very unusual Swansea watch to offer you. It never needs a battery or any winding. It has no hands, and no face of any kind."

"But how can you tell the time?"

"That's easy. Ask anybody."

As they say in Cardiff, drugs may be the road to nowhere, but at least they're the scenic route.

Swansea saying: Before you criticise someone, you should walk a mile in their shoes. That way you are a mile away from them and you have their shoes.

Swansea saying: If you lend someone £20 and never see that person again, it was probably worth it. So stab his brother.

Swansea saying: Dance like no one's watching.
   Cardiff saying: Don't dance. Everybody's watching.

Observation by a psychologist (a Bluebird): In Swansea people put the lights on first, then draw the blinds. In Cardiff they draw the blinds first, make sure that no one can see in, and then put the lights on.

A Jack stood watching a Bluebird fishing. He noticed that the man dipped his bait into a bottle by his side before each cast and was astounded to find that he had a dozen fine trout flapping on the bank beside him within five minutes. He became curious and went down to ask what his secret was.
   "No secret, but just a bottle of 50-year-old malt whisky. The fish just can't get enough of it."

So the man rushed back to his place and got out his own fishing rod. Oddly enough, he didn't have any 50-year-old malt whisky to hand so he decided to try out some of his freshly-bought bottle of Buckfast instead.

The next day the Bluebird was walking alongside the river and met the man coming the other way with a salmon the size of a small elephant slung over his shoulder.

He prudently restrained his natural curiosity regarding the existence of a fishing permit and said: "Congratulations. I'm glad to see the single malt whisky trick worked for you too."

The Jack grinned back and said: "You should try the electric soup instead. When I got this fish out of the water it took me five minutes to get the worm to let go of his throat."

8

JUST DESSERTS

A Jack and a Bluebird get into a car accident, and it's a bad one. Both cars are totally demolished, but amazingly, neither of them is hurt.

After they crawl out of their cars, the Bluebird says, "So you're a Jack, that's interesting. I'm a Bluebird. Wow! Just look at our cars. They're totally wrecked, but fortunately we're unhurt. This must be a sign from God that we should meet and be friends, putting our differences behind us."

The Jack replied, "I agree with you completely, this must indeed be a sign from God!" He continued, "And look at this – here's another miracle. My car is completely demolished but this bottle of whisky didn't break. Surely God wants us to drink this and celebrate our good fortune."

Then he hands the bottle to the Bluebird. He nods his head in agreement, opens it and takes a few big swigs from the bottle, then hands it back to the Jack. He takes the bottle, immediately

puts the cap back on, and hands it back to the Bluebird.

He asks: "Aren't you having any?"

The Jack grins and then replies, "No. I think I'll just wait for the cops."

9

JACKS AND DRINK

Cardiff (and Swansea) breakfast: A bottle of Buckfast, a big lump of laverbread and a spaniel. The spaniel is for eating the laverbread.

Swansea saying: There is no such thing as a large vodka.

The Jack doctor checked over his patient and said with a puzzled frown: "I can't really tell what the trouble is. I think it must be due to drink."

The patient said, understandingly: "Oh, that's all right doctor. I'll come back when you're sober."

In Swansea a seven course meal is a bottle of cider and six cans of beer.

Swansea saying: You aren't drunk if you can lie on the floor without holding on.

Swansea proverb: Never drink whisky without water and never drink water without whisky.

Three Cardiff men in a pub praising the beer:

First Bluebird: "Best glass of beer I never tasted no better."

Second Bluebird: "So did I neither."

Third Bluebird: "Neither did I too."

Jimmy the inebriate Jack was always coming home from the pub in the early hours of the morning.

Eventually he found this note from his wife: "The day before yesterday you came home yesterday morning. Yesterday you came home this morning. So if today you come home tomorrow morning you will find that I left you yesterday."

The same lady became a lodging-house keeper and wrote the following:

"I should like to know, please, whether you want two bedrooms with double beds in them, or two double-bedded rooms, as I have only one double-bedded room; all the beds are double beds except one in the double-bedded room, which is a single bed."

Having returned at 3 am from the office party, very much the worse for wear, Jimmy the inebriate Jack woke his wife with a dreadful noise.

She came downstairs to find him kicking the fridge and shouting: "The cash machine isn't working."

A man called at Jimmy the inebriate Jack's door collecting for the Home for Chronic Alcoholics.

His wife answered the door and said, "Call back after closing time. You can collect my husband then."

Jimmy the inebriate Jack arrived at Sadie's flat with a dozen cans of beer and a bottle of rum.

After half an hour of chat, Jimmy eventually asked: "When are the others coming for the party?"

Sadie looked surprised. "The party was last night. And you were here."

A Bluebird entered a bar and accidentally stood beside a Jack, who immediately initiated a conversation.

After they had chatted for a while the Jack asked: "Where are you from?"

The Bluebird replied, "I'm from the finest city in the world."

The Jack lowered his brows and said with that indefinable aura of menace: "Aye? That's not a Jack accent."

The pub was open again in a few days.

"Alcohol is your trouble," said the judge to Jimmy the inebriate Jack. "Alcohol alone is responsible for your present predicament."

Jimmy the inebriate Jack looked pleased as he said, "Thank you, judge. Everyone else says it's my fault!"

Alex the Jack told his friends that he couldn't come to the pub because his wife was doing bird imitations – she was watching him like a hawk.

Paddy the Jack decided to call his father-in-law "The Exorcist" because every time he came to visit he made the spirits disappear.

George the Jack's long-suffering Bluebird wife was fed up with her husband's unfortunate fondness of a not-so-small drink. Most evenings he would roll home from the pub considerably the worse for wear. His wife resolved to cure him. On Halloween, she put a bedsheet over her head, hid behind the hydrangea at the front door, and waited for her wayward man to come home. Eventually he staggered up the path.

His wife, in disguise, jumped out from behind the bushes, and cried out, "George! I'm the Devil! And I've come to warn you . . ."

"The Devil, are you?" George interrupted. "Then you must come in and have a drink with me. I do believe I'm married to your sister."

"Moderation, bach. Moderation is my rule. Nine or ten is reasonable refreshment, but after that it is likely to degenerate into drinking."
Anonymous, but definitely not a Bluebird.

And God said: "Let there be vodka!" And He saw that it was good and partook mightily.
Then God said: "Let there be light!"
And then He said: "Hold on, hold on – too much light."

To some it is just a bottle of Buckfast. To some Bluebirds it is an entire Social Work Department.

The problem with Cardiff people is that when they aren't drunk, they're sober.

Time is never wasted when you're wasted all the time.

Swansea saying: "24 hours in a day, 24 bottles in a case. Coincidence?"

Life is a waste of time, time is a waste of life, so get wasted all of the time and have the time of your life.

Reality is an illusion that occurs due to lack of alcohol.

If I had all the money I've spent on booze . . . I'd spend it on booze.

Buckfast is proof that God loves us and wants us to be happy.

The problem with Bluebirds is that they always seem to be a few drinks behind.

Give me a woman who loves beer and I will conquer the world.

You know you're drunk when you fall off the floor.

And, as Tom Waits so memorably said for most Jacks: "I'd rather have a bottle in front of me than a frontal lobotomy."

10

HEAVEN

A Cardiff couple on their way to get married were tragically killed in a terrible crash. Upon presenting themselves to St Peter at the gates to heaven, they asked if they could get married, specifying that they would like the ceremony carried out by a Bluebird priest.

"Give me some time," said St Peter, "and I'll check."

They waited and waited. After several months, they asked again.

"I'm working on it," said St Peter.

Months turned into years, then decades. Finally, after 30 years, St Peter came running to them. "OK, now you can get married!"

However, after a few months of married life, the couple really were not happy. They sought out St Peter and asked if there were divorces in heaven.

"Are you serious? It took me 30 years to find a Cardiff priest up here. I'll NEVER find a lawyer!"

A rich Bluebird lawyer was near death. He was very grieved because he had worked so hard stealing

people's money and he wanted to be able to take it with him to heaven. So he began to pray that he might be able to take some of his wealth with him.

A Jack angel hears his plea and appears to him. "Sorry, but you can't take your money with you."

The man implores the angel to speak to God to see if He might bend the rules.

The man continues to pray that his wealth could follow him. The angel reappears and informs the man that God has decided to allow him to take one suitcase with him. Overjoyed, the man gathers his largest suitcase and fills it with pure gold bars and places it beside his bed.

Soon afterward the man dies and shows up at the gates of Heaven to greet St Peter. St Peter, who by sheer coincidence is also a Jack, as is God, clocks the suitcase and says: "Hold on a minute, you can't bring that in here."

But the man explains to St Peter that he has permission and asks him to verify his story with the Lord. Sure enough, St Peter checks and comes back saying: "You're right. You are allowed one carry-on bag, but I'm supposed to check its contents before letting it through."

St Peter opens the suitcase to inspect the worldly goods that the man found too precious to

leave behind and says in surprise: "You brought pavement?"

A Bluebird dies and goes to heaven. He knocks on the pearly gates and out walks St Peter.

"Hello, mate," says St Peter, "I'm sorry, no Bluebirds in heaven."

"What?" exclaims the man, astonished.

"You heard, no Bluebirds."

"But, but, but, I've been a good man," replies the Bluebird.

"Oh really," says St Peter. "What have you done, then?"

"Well," said the guy, "three weeks before I died, I gave 10 pounds to the starving children in Africa."

"Oh," says St Peter, "anything else?"

"Well, two weeks before I died I also gave ten pounds to the homeless."

"Hmmm. Anything else?"

"Yeah. A week before I died I gave ten pounds to the Albanian orphans."

"Okay," said St Peter. "You wait here a minute while I have a word with the Big Man."

Ten minutes pass before St Peter returns. He looks the bloke in the eye and says, "I've had a word with God and he agrees with me. Here's your 30 quid back. Now fuck off."

A bus carrying only ugly Bluebirds and the only ugly Jack crashes into an oncoming truck, and everyone inside dies. They then get to meet their maker and, because of the grief they have experienced, he decides to grant them one wish each before they enter Paradise.

They're all lined up, and God asks the first one what the wish is.

"I want to be gorgeous," he says, so God snaps his fingers and it is done.

The second one in line hears this and says: "I want to be gorgeous too." Another snap of His fingers and the wish is granted.

This goes on for a while, but when God is halfway down the line, the Jack, who is the last in line, starts laughing. When there are only ten people left, this guy is rolling on the floor, laughing his bollocks off.

Finally, God reaches the guy and asks him what his wish will be. The Jack calms down and says: "Make them all ugly again."

A quiet looking young man knocks on the pearly gates and asks to be let in. St Peter says, "I don't know. Have you ever done anything good, like given money to the poor?"

"No," replied the man.

"Helped a widow or orphan?"

"No," replied the man.

"Helped a little old lady across a street?"

"No."

"Well then, why should I let you in?"

"I did do something very brave once," he said.

"And what was that?" asked St Peter.

"I went to Swansea on the train and ran around Swansea High Street station shouting: 'Jacks are all scumbags'."

"My, that is brave! When did you do that?"

"About three minutes ago."

St Peter was manning the Pearly Gates when 40 Jacks showed up. Never having seen any folk from Swansea at Heaven's door, St Peter said he would have to check with God. After hearing the news, God instructed him to admit the ten most virtuous from the group.

A few minutes later, St Peter returned to God breathless and said, "They're gone."

"What? All of the Jacks are gone?" asked God.

"Yes," replied St Peter, "and the Pearly Gates!"

11

HELL

Cardiff . . . because the Devil wanted a hell on earth.

One of the only two plumbers in Swansea to charge reasonable fees died and was sent to Hell by mistake. Eventually it was realised in Heaven that there was an honest Jack plumber in the wrong place so St Peter telephoned (on the hot line, naturally) to Satan.

"Have you got an honest plumber there?"

"Yes."

"He's ours, so can you send him up?"

"You can't have him!"

"Why not?"

"Because he's the only one who understands air conditioning. It's really cool down here now."

"Send him up at once," shouted St Peter, "or we'll sue."

"You'll sue?" laughed the voice at the other end. "And where will you get hold of a lawyer in Heaven? They're all either here or in Cardiff."

The preferred Jack way of dying: "I want to die peacefully in my sleep, like my grandfather. Not kicking and screaming like the passengers on his bus."

12

THE LIONS' SHARE

Here's an ancient story: Two Jacks were captured by the Romans and were thrown into a cell in the arena prior to being thrown to the lions. An instant friendship developed, as it does between Jacks, and they were chatting away amicably as they were led out in chains to the lions' den.

They were thrown in and one was asking the other: "So when is Gwyneth's baby due?" to receive the reply: "I'll tell you later. The lions are coming."

And there is another lions' den tale of a posse of Scumdiff kids on a bus trip to a safari park managing to escape from the bus, and their guardians, and prowl around outside among the animals.

A keeper, concerned for their safety, came running over, shouting: "The lions, boys, the lions!" to receive the reply: "We never touched your lions."

13

TERRORIST WARNING

Yesterday a friend was travelling on a Paris to Swansea flight. A man of Arabic appearance got off the plane and my friend noticed he had left his bag behind. She grabbed the bag and ran after him, caught up with him in the terminal and handed it to him.

He was extremely grateful and reached into the bag, which appeared to contain large bundles of money.

He looked around to make sure nobody was looking and whispered, "I can never repay your kindness, but I will try with words of advice for you: stay away from Cardiff!"

My friend was genuinely terrified. "Is there going to be an attack?" she asked him.

"No" he whispered back. "It's a shithole."

14

BLUEBIRDS AND MONEY

There's a modern twist to the old: "You'll have had your tea," Bluebird statement. Apparently nowadays they gesture toward the drinks cabinet and say: "Oh no, you'll be driving."

A Bluebird is someone who, after you have assured him or her that you have not had your tea and will not be driving, dribble you out a carefully measured modicum of cheap sherry, and when you say: "Stop," out of politeness, will do so.

A Jack, a Cockney and a Bluebird were in a bar and had just started on a new round of drinks when a fly landed in each glass of beer. The Jack took his out on the blade of his knife. The Cockney picked his out and put it in his pocket for later.

The Bluebird lifted his one up carefully by the wings and held it above his glass, saying: "Go on, spit it out."

A Bluebird lawyer opened the door of his BMW,

when suddenly a car came along and hit the door, ripping it off completely.

When the police arrived at the scene, the lawyer was complaining bitterly about the damage to his precious BMW.

"Officer, look what they've done to my Beeeeemer!" he whined.

"You lawyers are so materialistic, you make me sick," retorted the constable. "You're so worried about your stupid BMW that you didn't even notice that your arm was ripped off!"

"Oh no!" replied the lawyer, finally noticing the bloody right shoulder where his arm once was. "Where's my Rolex?"

Daryl the crafty Bluebird had become a bit hard of hearing, but he didn't want to pay for a hearing aid. So he bought a piece of flex, put one end in his top pocket and the other end in his ear. It didn't help his hearing but he found that people spoke to him more loudly.

A Bluebird and a Jack were sitting next to each other on an airplane. The Bluebird leans over to the Jack and asks if he wants to play a game. The Jack just

wants to sleep so he politely declines, turns away and tries to sleep.

The Bluebird persists and explains that it's a really easy game. He explains: "I ask a question and if you don't know the answer you pay me £5. Then you ask a question and if I don't know the answer I'll pay you £5." Again the Jack politely declines and tries to sleep.

The Bluebird, now somewhat agitated, says: "O.K., if you don't know the answer you pay me £5 and if I don't know the answer I pay you £50!" That got the Jack's attention, so he agrees to the game.

The Bluebird asks the first question: "What's the distance from the earth to the moon?" The Jack doesn't say a word and just hands the Bluebird £5.

Now, it's the Jack's turn. He asks the Bluebird: "What goes up a hill with three legs and comes down on four?" The Bluebird looks at him with a puzzled look, takes out his laptop, looks through all his references and after about an hour wakes the Jack and hands the Jack £50. The Jack politely takes the £50, turns away, and tries to return to sleep.

The Bluebird, a little miffed, asks: "Well, what's the answer to the question?" Without a word, the

Jack reaches into his wallet, hands £5 to the Bluebird, turns away, and returns to sleep.

A Bluebird matron, who was rather stingy, was giving a drink to a tradesman who had done a good job. As she handed him his glass, she said it was extra good whisky, being 14-years-old.

"Well, bach," said the man, regarding his glass sorrowfully, "It's very small for its age."

Gareth the careful Bluebird took his girlfriend out for the evening. They returned to her flat just before midnight and as she kissed him goodnight she said: "Be careful on your way home. I'd hate anyone to rob you of all the money you've saved this evening."

There was understandable scepticism when it was suggested that Napoleon Bonaparte was the grandson of a Bluebird. But now it has been pointed out that there is further proof that Napoleon was indeed from there – apart from being a little loser, his hand was always under his jacket, to make sure no one had lifted his wallet.

A visitor to a Cardiff bar was surprised to find the beer only two pence a pint. The barman explained that it was the price to mark the centenary of the

pub opening. The visitor noticed, however, that the bar was empty.

"Are the regular customers not enjoying the special prices?" he asked.

To which the barman replied: "They're waiting for the Happy Hour."

How do you persuade a Bluebird to go on the roof? Tell him the drinks are on the house.

When a bus company was prevailed upon to increase the concessionary fare to frequent travellers so that they got six journeys instead of four for a pound, one elderly gentleman, renowned for his frugality, even in a community where frugal folk are common, was still unhappy.

"It's all foolishness," he declared. "Now we've got to walk to town six times instead of four times to save a pound!"

Did you hear about the Bluebird who got caught making nuisance telephone calls? He kept reversing the charges.

Pat called in to see his Bluebird friend David to find he was stripping the wallpaper from the walls.

Rather obviously, he remarked, "You're decorating, I see."

To which David replied "No. I'm moving house."

If he had been a Jack he would have been kidding.

Have you heard the rumour that the Grand Canyon was started by a Bluebird who dropped a penny in a ditch?

Hear the one about the Bluebird who went out into the street the night before Christmas, blew up and burst a paper bag, and then told his kids that Santa had committed suicide?

Hear the one about the Bluebird who whispered to one of the Siamese twins, "Get rid of your sister, and I'll stand you a drink"?

Hear the one about the Bluebird who wrote to an editor, "If you don't stop printing derogatory jokes about mean-spirited Bluebirds, I'll stop borrowing your damn magazine"?

After discovering that they had won 15 million pounds in the Lottery, Mr and Mrs Bluebird sat down to discuss their future. Mrs Bluebird announced: "After 20 years of washing other

people's stairs, I can throw my old scrubbing brush away at last." Her husband agreed. "Of course you can, pet. We can easily afford to buy you a new one now."

Bluebirds have an infallible cure for sea-sickness. They lean over the side of the ship with a ten pence coin in their teeth.

In some Cardiff restaurants they heat the knives so you can't use too much butter. In Swansea restaurants the knives are chained to the tables. With very short chains.

It was a party. The Jack brought the Buckfast. The Irishman brought a crate of Guinness. The Scotsman brought a haggis. The Bluebird brought his brother.

What's the difference between a tightrope and a Bluebird?

A tightrope sometimes gives a little.

Bluebird lifestyle tip: Increase the life of your carpets by rolling them up and keeping them in the loft.

"Is old Mick a typical Bluebird?"

"Is he? He's saved all his toys for his second child-hood."

Bluebirds never smash in a face. They merely refrain from asking it to dinner.

The man who invented slow motion movies got the idea while watching a Bluebird reaching for the bill in a restaurant.

Bluebird savings tip:

Old telephone directories make ideal personal address books. Simply cross out the names and addresses of people you don't know.

The Bluebird was dying. On his deathbed, he looked up and said: "Is my wife here?"

His wife replies: "Yes, dear, I'm here, next to you."

The Bluebird goes: "Are my children here?"

"Yes, daddy, we are all here," say the children.

The Bluebird: "Are my other relatives also here?"

And they say: "Yes, we are all here . . . "

The Bluebird rears up in bed and says: "Then why is the light on in the kitchen?"

A Bluebird took a girl for a journey in a taxi. She was so beautiful he could hardly keep his eye on the meter.

Double glazing is doing great business in Cardiff and saving people a fortune. The kids can't hear the ice cream van when it comes round.

Three Bluebirds were in church one Sunday morning when the minister made a strong appeal for some very worthy cause, hoping that everyone in the congregation would give at least £10 or more. The three Bluebirds became very nervous as the collection plate neared them, and then one of them fainted and the other two carried him out.

A Jack was hopelessly lost in the hinterlands of Cardiff and wandered about for days, ending up in the Docks. Finally he caught the eye of an inhabitant, not always easy in the Docks.

"Thank heaven I've met someone," he cried. "I've been lost for ages."

"Is there a reward out for you?" asked the Bluebird.

"No," said the Jack.

"Then you're still lost," was the reply.

Did you hear about the last wish of the henpecked husband of a houseproud Bluebird wife? He asked to have his ashes scattered on the carpet.

A Bluebird was ill with measles. "Send for my creditors," he said. "At last I can give them something."

Did you hear about the Bluebird burglars who were arrested after a smash and grab raid?

They went back for the brick.

A Jack was being tried for being drunk and disorderly. The judge asked him where he had bought the bottle of vodka.

"I didn't buy it, Your Honour," said the Jack. "A Bluebird gave it to me."

"Fourteen days for perjury," said the judge.

What's the difference between a Bluebird and a coconut?

You can get a drink out of a coconut.

"Did anybody drop a roll of notes with an elastic band around them?" asked the Jack voice.

"Yes, I did," said several no-longer-quite-so-languid voices in the Cardiff bank queue.

"Well," said the Jack, "I just found the elastic band."

Why are 50p pieces the shape they are?

So you can use a spanner to get them off a Bluebird.

How do you tell you are in a Cardiff restaurant?

There's a fork in the sugar bowl.

The Bluebird put a penny in a weighing machine. A card came out which said, "You are a friendly spend-thrift."

It got his weight wrong too.

15

NEIGHBOURS

A Jack and a Bluebird lived next door to each other. The Jack owned a hen and each morning would look in his garden and pick up one of his hen's eggs for breakfast. One day he looked out and saw that the hen had laid an egg in the Bluebird's garden.

He was about to go next door when he saw the Bluebird pick up the egg. The Jack ran up to the Bluebird and told him that the egg belonged to him because he owned the hen. The Bluebird disagreed because the egg was laid on his property and, as we all know, they know about property. Sometimes they talk about something else, but not often and never for long.

Anyway, they argued for a while until finally the Jack smiled in that frightening way that they have and said: "In Swansea, we normally solve disputes by the following actions. I kick you in the groin and time how long it takes you to get back up, then you kick me in the groin and time how long it takes for me to get up. Whoever gets up quicker wins the egg."

The Bluebird agreed to this and so the Jack found his heaviest pair of boots and put them on. He took a few steps back, then ran toward the Bluebird and kicked him as hard as he could in the balls.

The Bluebird fell to the ground clutching his testicles, howling in agony for 30 minutes.

Eventually he stood up and said: "Now it's my turn to kick you."

At this the Jack said: "You just keep the egg."

The neighbour above was in the garden filling in a hole when his Bluebird neighbour peered over the fence.

Interested in what the man was up to, he politely asked: "What are you doing there?"

"My goldfish died," replied the Jack without looking up, "and I've just buried him."

The neighbour was very concerned. "That's an awfully big hole for a goldfish, isn't it?"

The Jack patted down the last heap of dirt then replied: "That's because he's inside your fucking cat."

In Cardiff lived a rich cat which was a bit of a snob, though she did deign to chat on occasion with her neighbour, a bin-raking tomcat from Swansea.

One day, she announced that she was about to have an operation, but she didn't mention what it was for.

Two weeks later, the Jack cat saw her again and inquired as delicately as he could how she was feeling, then dared to ask what kind of operation she had had.

"Oh, I am quite well now, thank you," the Bluebird cat replied, stiffly. "I had a hysterectomy."

"For God's sake!" the other cat exclaimed in exasperation: "Can you not just call a spayed a spayed."

16

ARCHITECTS

How many architects does it take to change a light bulb?

Architect's answer: Does it have to be a light bulb?

Cardiff answer: Does it have to be an architect?

Swansea answer: It's not those fuckers who built Legoland, is it?

"Any complaints?" asked the prison governor of the jailed Jack architect.

"Aye," replied Jimmy, "the walls are not built to scale."

17

BANTER

Swansea taxi driver's comment comparing the robustness of supermarket carrier bags: "FOUR bottles of booze in one Lidl bag! You're walking on eggshells, bach."

Jack to Bluebird: "Why is your beer like shagging in a canoe?"
   Bluebird: "Don't know, why?"
   Jack: "It's fucking close to water!"

The Jack beggar in Cardiff Central Station shambled over, holding out his filthy hand, and said: "Give a poor old blind man a pound, man."
   "But you can see out of one eye, I can see you doing it," said the Bluebird.
   "Everybody's a fucking critic, but let's be fair," said the Jack, "gimme 50p."

A Jack was recently flying to London. He decided to strike up a conversation with his seatmate.

"I've got a great Bluebird joke. Would you like to hear it?"

"I should let you know first that I am actually from Cardiff."

"That's OK. I'll tell it really slowly."

So I was getting into my car, and this Bluebird says to me: "Can you give me a lift?"

So I said, "Yeah, sure. You look great, the world's your oyster, go for it."

Phone answering machine message in your chav estate of choice in Cardiff (and it is a wide choice): "If you don't need to buy smack and it is just dope you want, press the hash key."

If you want to get served quickly in a Cardiff pub, learn to be polite. In Polish.

The token Jack woman is at the office night out in one of the few properly grungy bars left in Cardiff. She is very attractive and has had a few. She gestures alluringly to the barman, who comes over immediately. When he arrives, she seductively signals that he should bring his face closer to hers. When he

does so, she begins to gently caress his full beard, one of those annoying square-ended ones affected by Bluebird wankers, who think that it makes a difference.

"Are you the manager?" she asks, softly stroking his face with both hands.

"Actually, no," the man replies.

"Can you get him for me? I need to speak to him," she says, running her hands beyond his beard and into his hair.

"I'm afraid I can't," breathes the bartender. "Is there anything I can do?"

"Yes, there is. I need you to give him a message," she continues, slyly popping a couple of her fingers into his mouth and allowing him to suck them gently.

"What should I tell him?" the bartender manages to say.

"Please tell him," she whispers, "that there is no soap, toilet paper or towels in the ladies."

As Bill the Bluebird and Jimmy the Jack were coming out of the pub one afternoon, it started to rain very heavily.

"Do you think it will stop?" asked Bill.

"It always has," answered Jimmy.

A Jack goes into a pub in Cardiff and says, "Quick, gizza a beer before the trouble starts!" The barman looks around the sleepy pub, shrugs and hands the man a pint. The Jack quaffs it immediately.

"Quick! Gizza another beer before the trouble starts!" The barman looks at him oddly but pours him another pint. He again downs it immediately.

"Quick, another one before the trouble starts!" The barman draws him another beer, with a frown on his face, and hands it over reluctantly. Again, the Jack drinks it fast.

"Quick, another beer before the trouble starts!" The barman exasperatedly asks: "Look, exactly what trouble are you talking about?"

The Jack says: "I'm broke!"

18

A NEW JACK VERSION OF THE CLASSIC

Do, a beer, a Mexican beer.
Ray, a man who buys me beer.
Mi, I'd like to have a beer.
Fa, a long, long way for beer.
So, I think I'll have a beer.
La, la, la, la, la, la, beer!
Ti, no thanks, I'll have a beer.
And that brings us back to Do!

19

GOLF

It is now generally accepted that golf did not originate in Cardiff. No Bluebird would invent a game in which it was possible to lose a ball.

After the first hole, the Bluebird turned to his Jack opponent.

"How many did you take?" he asked.

"Eight," replied the Jack.

"I took seven, so that's my hole," said the Bluebird.

After the second hole, the Bluebird asked the same question. This time the Jack shook his head.

"No way," he replied, "it's my turn to ask first."

A Bluebird golf pro, after ten years of retirement, went back to the game. He'd found his ball.

20

FOOTBALL

Suggestion for a t-shirt:

Winning isn't everything.
  Beating Cardiff is.

The Cardiff City scouts have been scouring the country, offering their usual sweets and buttons for players and wages, but it is Knockback City all over the place. They finally find a youngster who looks very tasty and they get him along to the ground for a trial, where he puts on an astonishing display. He then confesses that the surroundings have made him play better as he is a lifelong Cardiff fan, and says that he will play for no wages.

He is hustled into the office for a quick physical, but the doc eventually, as everything else is looking good, goes: "Oh-oh."

"What's the matter?" asks the lad.

"You're Jewish, aren't you?" enquires the doc.

"Yes," he replies.

"Sorry, son, you'll not get a game here."

"Why not?" asks the affronted boy, sensing persecution.

"Jesus, son," sighs the doc, "everybody knows that you have to be a complete dick to play for City."

An Evertonian sharing a train up from London with a Swansea pal on their way to play Cardiff City and Man U was heard to comment: "No matter if we win or lose our games, we will still be winners in the game of life, because when they waken up tomorrow they'll still be from Cardiff and Manchester."

Cardiff City: A t-shirt and merchandising team, also plays football, but not nearly as well.

A new blue and white Oxo cube is about to be launched in the shops in both Swansea and Cardiff to recognise the achievements of both Everton and Man City. It will be called 'laughing stock'.

A 22-year-old secretary from Swansea was on holiday in Miami. However, as she walked along the beach eyeing the big-bosomed girls walking arm-in-arm with their boyfriends, she became distraught,

for she had a rather insignificant bosom herself. Suddenly, she spied a murky old bottle that had washed up on the beach, and for want of alternative amusement, picked it up. Poof! (Yes, they have them in Miami.) Out comes a genie, complete with flowing oriental robes, and immediately offered to grant her any two of anything that she desired.

"Give me a pair of the biggest tits in the whole, wide world," she moaned. Poof! Poof! (Yes, two of them.) Immediately there emerged, before her very eyes, Jay Bothroyd and Kevin McNaughton.

A Jack walked into a pub with a dog under his arm, just in time to hear the Saturday afternoon footie results on the telly.

"Swansea three, Cardiff nil," said the announcer, at which point the guy shouted: "Great!" and the dog shouted: "Oh no!" and started bawling his head off.

More than astonished, the barman leaned over the counter and said: "Eh, your dog just shouted 'Oh no!' "

"I know," said the dog's owner. "He always does that when Cardiff lose."

"What does he do when they win?" asked the barman.

"I don't know," said the Jack, with an evil smile, "I've only had him for a year and a half."

The same guy an hour or so later was waxing nostalgic about a previous pet: "My dog watched all the games. When Swansea won it jumped up and down and clapped its little paws. When we lost it used to do somersaults."

"You're kiddin', man. How many somersaults?" asked the impressed barman.

The Jack replied: "Depended how hard I kicked it."

A man, out walking his dog in a Cardiff street, came across an old bottle from which a genie appeared, offering the man a wish. (The usual way with bottles and genies in Cardiff. In Swansea you get three wishes.) Startled, the man asks if his dog could win at Crufts National Dog Show.

The genie looks at the flea-bitten, limping dog and replies, "I'm not a miracle worker. Think of another wish."

The fan then asks: "Can you get Cardiff City to win the Cup?"

The genie immediately says, "Let me have another look at your dog."

There are three kinds of football supporters in Wales:

First, there are the Bluebirds. They keep the Sabbath – and everything else they can lay their hands on. They pray on their knees . . . and their neighbours.

Second, there are the Jacks, who consider themselves self-made men, thus relieving God of a terrible responsibility.

Lastly, there are the rest, who never know what they want, but are willing to fight for it anyway, in between complaints in a very high-pitched nasal whine.

21

A NUMBER OF MAJOR EARTHQUAKES, MEASURING 3.2 ON THE RICHTER SCALE, HIT IN THE EARLY HOURS OF MONDAY 21ST OCTOBER 2008 EPICENTERED ON CARDIFF, UK

Victims can be seen wandering aimlessly in their estates with relatives, muttering in a sub-language called Goldie Lookin Chain Speak, which is not translatable into Welsh or English. The earthquake decimated the area, causing approximately £10 worth of damage. Subsequent to the seismic activity, some fireworks missed their intended human targets, causing damage to nearby historic and scientifically significant litter. It is estimated that, during the confusion, over £5 million worth of robbery-time was lost, damaging the Bluebirdunian economy.

Many were woken well before their giro arrived. Thousands are confused and bewildered, trying

to come to terms with the fact that something interesting has happened in Cardiff.

One resident, Donna-Marie Jones, a 17-year-old mother-of-three said: "It felt just like when the Jack Army came round one night. Little Chantal-Leanne came running into my bedroom shouting: 'fuck'. My youngest two, Liam-Noel and Kevin slept through it. I was still shaking when I was watching *Trisha* the next morning."

Apparently, though, looting did carry on as normal. The British Red Cross have so far managed to ship 4,000 crates of Buckfast to the area to help the stricken masses. Rescue workers are still searching through the rubble and have found large quantities of personal belongings including fireworks, burberry caps, benefit books and jewellery from Elizabeth Duke at Argos.

HOW YOU CAN HELP: This appeal is to raise clothing and food parcels for those unfortunate enough to be caught up in it. Clothing is most sought after. Items required include: caps, Adidas tracksuit bottoms, white socks, shell suits and boots.

Food parcels may be harder to put together but necessary all the same. Required foodstuffs include: pies, chips, McDonald's and beer.

Bluebirdunians have insisted: "to avoid problems with the social and tax authorities"(translation), they

don't need any more handouts but just wish to be able to "help themselves" in this difficult time, more than just the dole money they already claim (for five different people). £10 can provide a hammer, which can be used to batter grannies and back up shoplifting exploits, providing enough money to support a family of Bluebirds on McDonald's for the foreseeable future. £5 will provide a Bluebirdunian with essential E's and scag, 22p buys a biro for filling in a spurious compensation claim. If you can afford it, £120 buys a new pair of Nike Airs, justifying the chavs' decision to tuck their tracksuit bottoms into their socks, and helping said individual to avoid being caught while nicking said trainers from JD Sports.

Please do not send money directly to Bluebirdunians, as there is a good chance they'll come looking for you, realising in their primitive way, that where there is money to give away, there is great potential for robbery.

Please give generously. We know where you live.

22

CINDERELLA

Jack quick thinking (and a true story).

At Halloween a teenager in one of the nicer parts of Swansea (not telling) was reported by a curtain twitcher to be having sexual congress with a pumpkin in a front garden.

Here's the policewoman's account of what happened when she approached the young man.

"He was holding the pumpkin against the wall and I just went up and said, 'Excuse me, but you do realize that you are having sex with a pumpkin?' He froze and was clearly very surprised that I was there and then looked me straight in the face and said: 'A pumpkin? Christ . . . is it midnight already?' "

23

BLUEBIRDS AND SEX

An elderly man was walking through the French countryside, admiring the beautiful spring day, when over a hedgerow he spotted a young couple making love in a field. Getting over his initial shock, he said to himself: "Ah, young love . . . ze spring time, ze air, ze flowers . . . C'est magnifique!" and continued to watch, remembering good times.

Suddenly he drew in a breath and said: "Mais . . . Sacre bleu! Ze woman – she is dead!" and he hurried along as fast as he could to the town to tell Jean, the police chief. He came, out of breath, to the police station and shouted: "Jean . . . Jean zere is zis man, zis woman . . . naked in farmer Gaston's field making love."

The police chief smiled and said: "Come, come, Henri. You are not so old; remember ze young love, ze spring time, ze air, ze flowers? Ah, l'amour! Zis is okay."

"Mais non! You do not understand; ze woman, she is dead!"

Hearing this, Jean leapt up from his seat, rushed

out of the station, jumped on his bike, pedalled down to the field, confirmed Henri's story, and pedalled all the way back non-stop to call the doctor.

"Pierre, Pierre, this is Jean, I was in Gaston's field; zere is a young couple naked 'aving sex."

To which Pierre replied: "Jean, I am a man of science. You must remember, it is spring, ze air, ze flowers, Ah, l'amour! Zis is very natural."

Jean, still out of breath, gasped in reply, "NON, you do not understand; ze woman, she is dead!"

Hearing this, Pierre exclaimed: "Mon Dieu!" grabbed his black medicine bag; stuffed in his thermometer, stethoscope, and other tools; jumped in the car and drove like a madman down to Gaston's field. After carefully examining the participants he drove calmly back to Henri and Jean, who were waiting at the station.

He got there, went inside, smiled patiently, and said: "Ah, mes amis, do not worry. Ze woman, she is not dead, she is from Cardiff."

After having their tenth child, and finally finding out why this was happening, a couple from Cardiff decided that enough was enough. The husband went to his doctor and told him that he and his wife didn't want to have any more children. The doctor

told him that there was a procedure called a vasectomy that could fix the problem. The doctor told the man that he was to go home, get a firework, put it in a can, then hold the can up to his ear and count to 10.

The man said to the doctor "I may not be the smartest man, but I don't see how putting a banger in a can next to my ear is going to help me."

So the couple drove to Swansea to get a second opinion. The doctor was just about to tell them about the procedure for a vasectomy when he noticed they were from Cardiff. This doctor also told the man to go home and get a banger, place it in a tin can, hold it next to his ear and count to 10.

Figuring that both doctors couldn't be wrong, the man went home, lit a firework and put it in a can. He held the can up to his ear and began to count, "One, two, three, four, five . . ." at which point he paused, placed the can between his legs and resumed counting on his other hand . . .

A young Bluebird was all set up for his very first sexual experience, but his girlfriend says: "Sorry Dai, not without a condom."

He is totally skint and walking disconsolately around, knowing better than to ask anyone in

Cardiff for money, when he eventually meets Old Jess, a very good friend of his father.

Young Dai explains his problem and is told in return: "Don't worry son, I can help you out." He vanishes for a moment and returns with a condom.

Dai takes off and the night is beyond his wildest expectations. A week later, he meets Old Jess in the street and tells him about his experience.

"It was wonderful, Jess. Thanks to you, I had the best time I have ever had."

"Just glad I could help out, son; now where's the condom?" asked Old Jess.

Dai looks at him and replies: "I threw it away."

Old Jess, with a scowl on his face says, "Ah, you are in trouble now, boy. That condom belonged to the club."

24

NUTTY STORIES

A Jack in Cardiff for the footie goes into a restaurant and orders a carry-out. While he waits, he grabs a handful of peanuts from the bowl on the counter, and as he starts to chew he hears a voice say: "That's a beautiful shirt, is that silk? Very nice choice!"

Wondering who made the comment, and mindful of all the advice he has had regarding Bluebirds' sexual proclivities, he looks around and doesn't see anyone nearby who could be speaking to him. With a shrug, he pops a few more peanuts into his mouth.

Next he hears the voice say: "That is a lovely pair of shoes, bach. Are they Italian leather? They look great!"

A little worried, the man decides to move away and play the slot machine. As he puts a coin in the one-armed bandit he hears a harsh voice say: "You ugly Jack prick." He looks around but there's still no one there.

A couple of seconds later the second voice says: "Fuck off, you smelly Swansea tosser!"

At this, the man called the bartender in the restaurant over. "Hey, I must be goin' off my head," he told the bartender. "I keep hearing these voices, one saying poofy things, and one noising me up, and there's not a soul in here but us. If you are a ventriloquist, you are dead."

"No, no, no," answered the bartender. "That's the peanuts . . . they're complimentary, but the bandit's well out of order."

A Bluebird in his mid-40s goes looking for a job on a building site in Swansea. On meeting the foreman, he enquires about any vacancies he may have.

"Aye, well, I've just had to let someone go, so I'm a man down. Do you have any experience?"

The man pauses and looks anxious before telling him of his work history.

"Well, you see, I've been involved in major construction work all my life, but I was involved in an accident a couple of years ago and haven't worked since."

"What happened?" the foreman enquired.

"Well, to cut a long story short, I was working with a large industrial saw when it slipped and . . . unfortunately, I castrated myself."

"Ouch!" the foreman said, wincing at the thought and studiously avoiding jokes about Bluebirds

having no balls anyway. "Right, you obviously have loads of experience otherwise, so come down tomorrow morning at nine and I'll get you started."

"That's great," said the man, "but don't you and your crew start work at eight?"

The foreman nods and, with a very Jack grin says: "Aye, but we just stand about scratching our balls for the first hour."

25

CARDIFF CORRUPTION

Cardiff Council rule: If two wrongs don't make a right, try three.

Trying to find an honest man in Cardiff is like trying to find a fart in a Jacuzzi.

Cardiff Council: so many fiddles going on that they hired Yo Yo Ma to conduct them.

It is a miracle that curiosity survives any formal education, especially the Cardiff private school model, which may well have given rise to the saying: Swansea people want to know, Cardiff people think they know already.

Cardiff bureaucrats: A difficulty for every solution.

26

LITTLE DARLINGS

At Cherrylaurellaburnum Primary, in one of the nicer parts of Cardiff, Miss Fotheringill is asking the good little boys and girls of first year what their fathers do, so that the headmistress can mark out the future prefects.

"My daddy is a judge, Miss Fotheringill," says little Samantha, brushing back the royal blue bow which holds her mane of freshly-washed blonde locks.

"Very good, Samantha dear," says Miss Fotheringill, placing a discreet tick beside little Samantha's name in her big black book before moving on to the desk of little Roland.

"My daddy's a consultant surgeon, Miss Fotheringill," says little Roland, his big blue eyes filled with the innocence of freshly cut church lawns.

"That's very nice, Roland dear," says Miss Fotheringill, marking little Roland down as a future head boy and moving on to the desk of little Ieuan, whose father was a Swansea bookie who won the lottery and whose mother is a poisoner. Miss

Fotheringill does not know this, but the tattoos of swallows flitting across little Ieuan's neck and up under his ear has already drawn her to the conclusion that little Ieuan is definitely not future officer material. Nevertheless, she asks the same question of him.

"My dad's dead," says little Ieuan.

"Oh dear," says Miss Fotheringill, overcome with remorse for her unkind thoughts about the poor lad. "And what did he do before he died, little Ieuan?"

"He grabbed his throat and went 'Aaaarrrrggghhhh', Miss."

Little Swansea Tommy was sitting on a park bench on a day out in Cardiff munching on one deep-fried Mars Bar after another.

After the sixth one a Bluebird on the bench across from him said, "Son, you know eating all that fat and chocolate isn't good for you. It will give you acne, rot your teeth, and make you fat."

Little Swansea Tommy replied, "My grandfather lived to be 107-years-old."

The man asked, "Did your grandfather eat six Mars Bars at a time?"

Little Swansea Tommy answered, "No, he minded his own fucking business!"

My mum and dad are Jacks but they moved to Cardiff when I was two and then sent me to a private school, because they wanted me to sound like an arsehole.

A pupil told his registration teacher that he would not be in on Friday because he was going to his sister's wedding. When he returned the following Monday the teacher asked him how it had gone. He also remembered that the boy's father was dead and asked him if he had given the bride away.

The latter replied: "I could have, but I kept my mouth shut. I grass no one."

27

DEAD BLUEBIRDS. THERE AREN'T ENOUGH OF THEM.

A Bluebird went to live in Swansea but unfortunately (kind of) he died. Two Jacks went around from house to house collecting money to give him a decent funeral.

"Excuse me," they asked up one close, "would you contribute even just 50 pence to bury a Cardiff man?"

"Yeh," said the Jack, "here's £10 – bury 20 of them."

A Jack and a Bluebird were travelling on a motorcycle through windy countryside. When it became too breezy for one of them, he stopped and put his overcoat on backward to keep the wind from ballooning it away from him. A few miles further down the road, the motorcycle hit a tree, killing the driver and stunning the man with the reversed coat. Later, when the Superintendent visited the scene,

he said to the policeman standing nearby: "What happened?"

"Well," the young policeman replied, "one of them was dead when I got here, and by the time I got the head of the lad from Cardiff straightened out, he was dead too."

A Bluebird woke up one morning to find his wife cold and stiff beside him. And she was dead as well. He jumped from his bed and ran, horror-stricken, into the kitchen.

"Marisa," he said breathlessly to the au pair.

"Si, si," she cried. "What is it? Que pasa?"

"Just one egg for breakfast this morning."

The insurance man knocked lightly on the door of the Cardiff semi-detached. The widower, his black suit contrasting with his pale white features, opened it very slowly. He ushered the insurance man into the living room, where two (very small) glasses of sherry were poured. They sat in silence until the insurance man dug into his briefcase and then in a very quiet voice said: "Everything is in order, Mr.Evans. Here is our cheque for £500,000."

Evans stared at the cheque: "Five hundred thousand," he muttered. "Five hundred thousand pounds

for a life of goodness, love, faith, devotion and charity. You know," (and here he stopped to wipe away a tear), "I'd gladly give half of this back to have Margaret alive today."

A Jack stopped before a grave in a Cardiff cemetery, containing a tombstone declaring: "Here lies a Cardiff lawyer and an honest man."

"And who would ever think," he murmured, "there would be room enough for two men in that one small grave."

28

IT'S THE ACCENT

A young Jack woman was on her first Mediterranean cruise and was talking to a Bluebird matron who somewhat snobbishly announced that she had been on many, concluding by saying in that whiny Bluebird way: "My Gareth works for Cunard."

The Jill looked at her and said: "This might just be our first cruise, but my man works fuckin' 'ard as well."

A Bluebird was made ashamed of his accent when working in Cardiff so he went South to get elocution lessons. He returned three years later, speaking perfect Queen's English, and went out to celebrate with a drink, walking into the first establishment he could find.

"I say, my good man," his silky tones rang out, "perhaps you could find me a bottle of chilled Bolly and one of your finest Havana cigars."

"You're from Butetown, aren't you," said the proprietor.

"Good Lord, how ever did you possibly know?" asked the stunned and aggrieved man.

"Well, you see," said the proprietor, "this is a butcher's."

29

A WORD TO THE WISE

An old Jack is wandering about Cardiff city centre for ages looking for a friendly face and a place for a bite that doesn't take a mortgage to fund. He sees a young barman having a fag outside a pub and the young guy gives him a friendly smile and a nod, as he is a Jack too. Delighted, the old guy goes into the pub and is served by the young guy.

The pensioner asks for a bowl of soup and smiles up at the young guy and says: "And maybe a kind word as well, lad?"

The young guy brings the soup and as he is turning away the old guy catches his sleeve and says: "And the kind word?"

The young Jack leans over and whispers in his ear: "Don't eat the soup."

30

SILLY, BUT NOT STUPID

There was a Jack living in Cardiff who always hung around a supermarket owned by a Bluebird. The owner, Tim, doesn't know what Jimmy's problem is, but the local boys like to tease him. They say he is two bricks shy of a load, or two pickles short of a ploughman's lunch. To prove it, sometimes they offer Jimmy his choice between a pound and a 50 pence piece. He always takes the 50 pence, they say, because it's bigger.

One day after Jimmy grabbed the 50 pence piece, Tim got him off to one side and said, "Those boys are making you out to be a fool. They think you don't know the pound is worth more than the 50p. Are you grabbing the 50p because it's bigger, or what?"

Jimmy said, "Well, if I took the £1, they'd stop doing it, wouldn't they?"

31

CANNIBALLOCKS

A Jack, a Bluebird and a Londoner were captured by cannibals. The chief comes to them and says: "The bad news is that now we've caught you and we're going to kill you. We will put you in a pot, cook you, eat you and then we're going to use your skins to build a canoe. The good news is that you can choose how to die."

The Bluebird says: "Give me a case of gin and a few bottles of tonic," then retires to his hut and after a few choruses of: "Cardiff till I die!", drinks himself to death and is duly skinned, cooked, eaten, and turned into a canoe.

The Londoner says: "Brandy for me please, might as well go the expensive way. And a little ginger ale."

The chief gives him the brandy and the mixer, and after a few renditions of: "Chelsea for ever!" duly expires and is skinned, cooked etc.

The Jack says: "A crate of vodka and a fork. No mixer necessary."

The chief is puzzled, but he shrugs and gives him the vodka and the fork. The Jack takes them and

goes to his hut. Later the chief goes to see him and there he is, half of the vodka gone, broken bottle in one hand, fork in the other, jabbing himself all over . . . the stomach, the sides, the chest, everywhere. There is blood gushing out, it's horrible.

The chief is appalled and asks: "My God, what are you doing?"

And the Jack responds, as he sticks the broken bottle in the chief's face: "Fuck you AND your canoe!"

32

THE LORD GOD AND BLUEBIRDS

A Swansea prayer: "Oh Lord, we do not ask you to give us wealth. Just show us where it is."

A Cardiff prayer: "Oh Lord, we do not ask you to give us wealth. Just show us where the Jacks are."

Eric the Bluebird finds himself in dire trouble. His business has gone bust and he's got serious financial problems. He's so desperate that he decides to ask God for help.

"God, please help me. I've lost my store and if I don't get some money, I'm going to lose my house too. Please let me win the lottery."

Lottery night. Someone else wins.

Eric prays again. "God, please let me win the lottery! I've lost my store, my house and I'm going to lose my car as well."

Lottery night again! Still no luck. Eric prays again.

"I've lost my business, my house and my car. My little ones are starving. I don't often ask You for help and I have always been a good servant to You.

PLEASE just let me win the lottery this one time so I can get back on my feet!"

Suddenly there is a blinding flash as the heavens open and the voice of God Himself thunders, in a very Jack accent: "Give me a break here, Eric. Meet Me halfway, you miserable, moanin' Bluebird twat. Buy a ticket!"

An evil atheist Bluebird explorer in the deepest Amazon suddenly finds himself surrounded by a bloodthirsty group of natives. Upon surveying the situation, he says quietly to himself: "Oh God, I'm fucked."

There is a ray of light from heaven and a Jack voice booms out: "No, evil atheist, you are NOT fucked. Pick up that stone at your feet and bash in the head of the chief standing in front of you."

So the explorer picks up the stone and proceeds to turn the chief's head to mince.

As he stands above the lifeless body, breathing heavily and surrounded by 100 natives with a look of shock on their faces, God's voice booms out again: "Right lad, NOW you're fucked."

33

OPPORTUNITIES

There was a Jack, a Bluebird and Sharon Stone sitting together in a train. Suddenly the train went through a tunnel and, as it was an old-style steam train, there were no lights in the carriages and it went completely dark. Then there was this kissing noise and the sound of a really loud slap. When the train came out of the tunnel, Sharon Stone and the Jack were sitting as if nothing had happened and the Bluebird had his hand against his face going: "Ouch!"

The Bluebird was thinking: "The Jack must have kissed Sharon Stone and she missed him and slapped me instead."

Sharon Stone was thinking: "The Bluebird must have tried to kiss me and actually kissed the Jack and got slapped for it."

And the Jack was thinking: "This is great. The next time the train goes through a tunnel I'll make that kissing noise and slap that Bluebird again."

A Jack and a Bluebird are strolling along Blackpool

beach when they find a lamp. They clean it up and out pops a genie.

"I'll give you each one wish (it's a Cardiff genie) for anything you want," says the genie.

The Bluebird thinks then says, "I believe in Cardiff for the folk of Cardiff. I'm sick and tired of all these Jacks coming to MY city, driving property values down, laughing, drinking and winning at football. I wish for a huge wall around Cardiff to keep the Jacks out."

POOF! (It is still Cardiff) and it's done. The Jack has a think.

"Genie?" he says "tell me about this wall."

"Well," says the genie, "it's 500 feet high, a third of a mile thick, nothing can get in and nothing can get out."

"OK," says the Jack: "Fill it with water."

A Jack is walking along the beach when he discovers an old bottle. He takes the cork out of it and a genie appears.

The genie says: "I'll grant you three wishes (it is a Jack genie), but whatever you wish for, the Bluebirds will receive double."

"Ok," says Jimmy: "My first wish is for a million pounds."

The genie says: "Ok, but the Bluebirds will receive two million."

"No problem," says the Jack, "I can live with that."

"My second wish is that Swansea win the Cup."

Again, the genie says: "That's fine, but Cardiff will win the next two after that."

The Jack shakes his head but agrees: "Ok, I can live with that."

"What is your third wish?" asks the genie.

"Well," said the Jack slowly, "I'd like to donate a kidney."

34

WHAT'S IN A NAME?

A Bluebird and his partner were driving their fuck-off sized Recreational Vehicle and were nearing Swansea.

Justin said to Cammie: "It's pronounced Swansseee or something like that."

Cammie demurred, a thing Cardiff lawyers do a lot of.

Since they were hungry, they pulled into a place to get something to eat. At the counter, Justin said to the waitress: "Cammie and I can't seem to be able to agree on how to pronounce this place. We're from Cardiff. Will you tell me where we are and say it very slowly so that I can understand."

The waitress looked at him and said: "Buuurrrgerrr Kiiiinnnng."

35

NEW SIMPLIFIED FORM FOR 2009 SWANSEA COUNCIL TAX

1. Calculate how much money you made in 2009.
2. Send it to us.

36

SWANSEA'S FINEST

On Christmas morning a policeman on horseback is heading for the major Christmas present resettlement area that is Butetown. He is sitting at a traffic light and next to him is a little boy on a shiny new bike.

The cop says to the kid, "Nice bike you've got there. Did Santa steal that for you?"

The boy says, "Yes."

The cop says, "Well, next year tell Santa to put a light on that bike."

The cop then proceeds to issue the kid a bicycle safety order, meaning that he has to turn up at the police station.

The boy takes the chit and before he rides off says, "By the way, that's a nice horse you've got there. Did Santa bring that to you?"

Humouring the kid, the policeman says: "Yes, that he did."

The boy says: "Well, next year tell Santa to put the prick underneath the horse."

Swansea Police, MI5, and a secret Government department are all trying to prove that they are the best at apprehending criminals. The Prime Minister decides to give them a test. He releases a rabbit into a forest and each of them has to catch it.

MI5 goes in. They place animal informants throughout the forest. They question all plant and mineral witnesses. After three months of extensive investigations they conclude that rabbits do not exist.

The ultra-secret Government department goes in. After two weeks with no success they poison the forest with some mysterious substance, killing nearly everything in it, and they make no apologies. Nobody ever mentions their failure. Or their existence. A bit like Masons in the police force.

Swansea's finest go in. They come out two hours later with a Rottweiller that is showing a bit of wear and tear. It is limping on all four legs and pissing blood, but there are of course no visible injuries.

The dog is yelling: "Okay! Okay! I'm a rabbit! I'm a rabbit!"

A Jack and a Bluebird were stopped by the police for being drunk and disorderly. It turned out that the first had been drinking battery acid and the second had been swallowing fireworks.

The Jack was charged and the Bluebird was let off. The desk sergeant got a rocket for not prosecuting him.

Real quote from a Swansea policeman: "Relax, the handcuffs are tight because they're new. They'll stretch after you wear them for a while."

A Jack candidate for the Cardiff police force was being verbally examined.

"If you were by yourself in a police car and were pursued by a desperate gang of criminals doing 60 mph. What would you do?"

The Jack looked puzzled at the simplicity of the question, then replied, "70."